The Inspired Vegetarian

The Inspired Vegetarian

LOUISE PICKFORD

Photographs by Gus Filgate

STEWART, TABORI & CHANG

NEW YORK

To my parents, John and Elizabeth,

and to my husband, Ian.

Front cover: Baked Baby Vegetables with Citrus
Back cover: Chocolate Mousse Terrine with Pistachio Sauce

Text copyright © 1992 Louise Pickford
Photographs copyright © 1992 Gus Filgate
Edited by Ann ffolliott

Published in 1992 by
Stewart, Tabori & Chang, Inc.
575 Broadway, New York, New York 10012

Library of Congress Cataloging-in-Publication Data

Pickford, Louise.
The inspired vegetarian / by Louise Pickford ; photographs by Gus
Filgate.
p.   cm.
Includes index.
ISBN 1-55670-230-2
1. Vegetarian cookery.   I. Title.
TX837.P5285   1992
641.5'636—dc20   92-9094
CIP

Distributed in the U.S. by Workman Publishing,
708 Broadway, New York, New York 10003
Distributed in Canada by Canadian Manda Group,
P.O. Box 920 Station U, Toronto, Ontario M8Z 5P9

Printed in Japan

10 9 8 7 6 5 4 3 2 1

Contents

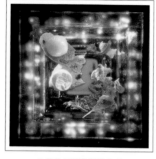

APPETIZERS

SOUPS

MAIN COURSES

VEGETABLE
ACCOMPANIMENTS

SALADS

BREADS

DESSERTS

Introduction

THE INSPIRED VEGETARIAN is a collection of my favorite vegetarian recipes, aimed at those people who share my passion for fresh vegetables, herbs, and fruits. I hope it will also encourage the reluctant vegetarian, who up until now has been convinced that there is little more to vegetarian food than lentil stews, veggie burgers, tofu, and whole wheat pastry. After all, just because vegetarians prefer not to eat meat or fish, that is no reason to assume nonvegetarians cannot also enjoy recipes without them. And we are continually being advised to cut down on our consumption of meat—especially red meat— to improve our health.

My own conversion to vegetables was sudden and quite dramatic. As a child I had refused to eat any vegetables except peas, beets, and raw carrots despite being surrounded by fresh, homegrown produce. It was through my career as a food stylist that I came, very late, to the delights of all the wonderful vegetable dishes there are. As I began to spend my time preparing and presenting food for photography, I was exposed to nearly all the world's cuisines. As my passion for food grew, I began to create my own recipes, some for publication but many more for my personal pleasure.

It was at this time that I discovered my latent love of vegetables, and I was somewhat surprised and disappointed by the lack of innovative vegetarian cookbooks. I wanted to learn about new and exotic dishes, not be told that vegetarians had to limit their diet to rather heavy, unexciting stews, mock-meat patties, and casseroles. I found myself referring to the vegetable dishes of such renowned cookbook writers as Jane Grigson, Elizabeth David, Paula Wolfert, Giuliano Bugialli, and Claudia Roden for my inspirations. I decided that I wanted to pursue a more modern approach to vegetarian cuisine by compiling a collection of my favorite recipes and presenting them in a way that would inspire a new generation of passionate cooks.

I began working with the photographer Gus Filgate, whose pictures are quite extraordinary in their quality and creativity as well as evocative of his love of the food that is his model.

Such classics as French onion soup, *soupe au pistou*, and cassoulet inspired me to create vegetarian alternatives for the modern cook. In turn, Gus's photographs emphasize this mood by their originality.

The recipes have been divided into chapters, so full-course meals can easily be assembled. The chapter divisions are, however, just my suggestions. In some cases I have given suggestions for combinations of dishes that I feel work well together for a successful balance of flavors, textures, and nutritional content.

The first chapter presents the appetizers. These recipes were developed to tempt the appetite and prepare the taste buds for the next delicious course.

To follow are ten very different soups, ranging from light fragrant summer soups to a rich vegetable broth. These can be served as an appetizer, a soup course, or a lunch or light supper dish, accompanied by one of the breads.

Many of the main courses, such as the Spiced Vegetable Pakoras with Mango Relish *(page 60)* or Tipsy Parsnips *(page 52)* have complex flavors and are best served with either simply cooked vegetables or a light salad.

The vegetable accompaniments and salads are ideal for serving as part of a larger, buffet-style meal. Alternatively, serve them with one of the simpler main courses, such as the Layered Vegetable Terrine *(page 64)* or the Warm Mushroom Salad *(page 72)*.

A short bread chapter provides a good selection of interesting and wholesome breads with a variety of flavors and textures. My particular favorite is the rolled and stuffed Sun-Dried Tomato and Parmesan Bread *(page 114)*.

What better way to end a perfect meal than with one of the delicious desserts, ranging from the fresh-tasting Pear and Blackberry Sorbet with Vodka *(page 120)* to the rich and creamy Chocolate Mousse Terrine with Pistachio Sauce *(page 124)*.

I hope that in producing this book, which has been great fun, we will inspire others to share our enthusiasm in creating new ideas for all forms of vegetarian cooking.

Practical Matters

It is my belief that good cooking is a matter of confidence in your own judgment. Because there are so many determining factors involved in cooking—the pans used, the stove, the ingredients, and even the environment in which they are cooked—it is important to exercise this judgment to make successful decisions.

I want the recipes in this book to inspire you and encourage you to experiment with my ideas to suit your own particular tastes, rather than strictly following the recipes. For example, if preparing a recipe takes you a little longer or a little less time than stated, trust your instincts and act accordingly.

The addition of seasonings to a dish is also a very personal aspect of cooking. To be sure, "some like it hot," but others do not, and I recommend that while you are cooking, you taste the food at every stage and after each new addition. This enables you to make an informed decision and add a little more or a little less seasoning according to your own taste.

Herbs and spices should be added with care. They add depth of flavor to a dish, but they should be used with a light hand so they do not overpower the other ingredients. Remember, freshly ground spices taste sharper and stronger than those that have been ground previously, and fresh herbs have a more defined flavor than dried. Consider these points before deciding which recipes you will prepare and the resulting dishes will be more successful.

When it comes to using fresh ingredients, start by determining what is really in season and use only the freshest foods available. After all, if you start with poor-quality produce, no amount of coercing or pleading will make the dish other than disappointing.

In addition to fresh ingredients, consider the staples you will also need. Buy good-quality oils, vinegars, dried beans, and nuts. If possible make your own vegetable stock, which will add a better balance of flavor to your soups or sauces. I've included a versatile stock recipe that can be used for many recipes *(page 45)*.

Do not become disheartened at these strictures because a good cook's true success is determined by his or her love and enjoyment of cooking. Shopping for the food; washing and sorting the vegetables; chopping and grinding the herbs, spices, and nuts;

frying, broiling, and roasting the vegetables; serving the meal, and eating and appreciating dishes so lovingly prepared are all part of this ritual so central to all of our lives.

A Little About the Ingredients

· Yogurt cheese, also known as strained yogurt, is made by removing some of the water from plain yogurt. Simply suspend the yogurt in a double thickness of cheesecloth or a clean coffee filter over a bowl and let it drain for an hour or two, until the desired consistency is reached.

· Nuts should be toasted in a preheated 400°F. oven as follows:
—whole nuts for 10 to 12 minutes
—chopped nuts for 8 to 10 minutes
—ground nuts for 5 minutes

· Dried herbs can be substituted for fresh herbs.
1 tablespoon chopped fresh herbs = 1 teaspoon dried

· Filo dough is usually sold frozen and should be thawed to room temperature before use. Check package instructions on refreezing. It dries out very quickly when exposed to air, so keep it well covered with a sheet of wax paper and a damp towel until required.

· Recipes use lightly salted butter unless otherwise stated.

· Recipes use large eggs unless otherwise stated.

· Olive oil should always be of good quality, preferably extra-virgin or virgin.

· Always use freshly ground salt and pepper.

· Always buy the freshest seasonal produce.

· Always preheat your oven before baking.

I hope you have as much enjoyment using the recipes in this book as I have had creating them.

Acknowledgments

BOTH GUS AND I are greatly indebted to Leslie Stoker for her trust, encouragement, and continual enthusiasm throughout the duration of this project. To Gus, of course, I give many thanks for his beautiful photographs and his patience.

I would also like to thank Ann ffolliott, who edited the book, which was no easy task with the Atlantic Ocean between us. A huge thanks must go to Lynn Pieroni, who designed the book so beautifully.

My thanks also go to my team of testers, Joanne Olney, Rebecca Money, and Elizabeth Pickford, with special thanks to Frances Cleary for both her enthusiastic comments and her help with Americanizations.

Thank you to my fruit and vegetable suppliers, Hyams and Cockerton, and to City Herbs, for their cooperation in supplying me with the more exotic produce, and to Janine at China & Co. for her help in supplying many of the beautiful props.

Finally, both Gus and I would like to thank Ian and Suzanne, for their support and understanding of the sometimes erratic behavior of author and photographer.

Marinated Goat Cheese

I began marinating cheeses, including goat cheeses, several years ago, with great success. Goat cheeses absorb the flavors from the marinade, which can be made with an endless variety of aromatics. Once sealed, store the jars in a cool place (but not the refrigerator) for at least one week, but not more than four. The cheeses tend to soften after a while.

Ingredients

6 small goat cheeses, about 1½ ounces each	1 teaspoon coriander seeds, bruised
2 small red or green chilies	1 teaspoon cumin seeds, bruised
2 cloves garlic, peeled but left whole	2 strips lemon zest
2 sprigs of thyme	2 cups extra-virgin olive oil
2 sprigs of rosemary	Freshly ground black pepper

Place the cheeses in a wide-necked sterile jar and add the chilies, garlic, thyme, rosemary, coriander, cumin, lemon zest, olive oil, and pepper. Cover tightly and set aside to marinate.

Serve the cheeses with slices of toasted Olive and Pine Nut Bread *(page 113)* and a garnish of salad greens.

Eggplant Pâté with Minted Yogurt Dressing

SERVES 6

Baking eggplants whole in the oven results in the flesh being creamy and full of the vegetable's natural flavor. The flesh is then blended with spices and sesame paste for a rich pâté, which is served with mint and yogurt sauce.

Ingredients

PATE	DRESSING
2 medium eggplants	⅓ cup plain yogurt
1 tablespoon olive oil	1 tablespoon peanut oil
1 medium onion, finely chopped	1 teaspoon white wine vinegar
2 cloves garlic, crushed	2 teaspoons chopped fresh mint
1 tablespoon chopped fresh coriander (cilantro)	Salt and freshly ground black pepper
1 teaspoon ground cumin	Olives and coriander leaves, for garnish
Pinch of cayenne pepper	
1 tablespoon sesame paste (tahini)	
1 tablespoon lemon juice	

Preheat the oven to 400°F. Prick the eggplants with a fork and bake for 25 to 30 minutes, or until the flesh feels soft to the touch. Remove from the oven, cool slightly, then peel and mash the flesh.

Heat the olive oil in a skillet and sauté the onion and garlic for 5 minutes. Add the coriander, cumin, and cayenne and stir-fry for 2 to 3 minutes. Puree with the mashed eggplant, sesame paste, and lemon juice until smooth and season to taste. Let cool, then refrigerate until required.

Blend the yogurt, peanut oil, vinegar, mint, and salt and pepper and set aside for 1 hour to allow the flavors to infuse.

To serve, form the pâté into ovals and place 2 on each serving plate. Pour over a little dressing and garnish with olives and coriander.

Stuffed Filo Triangles

SERVES 6

Filo dough is a paper-thin pastry used throughout the eastern Mediterranean region to make both sweet and savory pastries. In this recipe the filo dough is cut into strips that are rolled into small triangles folded with a savory cheese, spinach, and mint stuffing. The triangles are served with a strawberry and olive salad—an exotic combination.

Ingredients

2 large sheets filo dough

FILLING
1 tablespoon olive oil
1 clove garlic, crushed
1 medium leek,
trimmed and thinly sliced
3 cups packed spinach leaves,
thinly shredded
2 tablespoons chopped fresh mint

1 teaspoon ground cumin
½ cup (4 ounces) crumbled feta cheese
¼ cup (2 ounces) ricotta or
double-cream cheese
⅓ cup chopped walnuts
1 teaspoon lemon zest
1 tablespoon lemon juice
6 tablespoons (¾ stick)
unsalted butter

Remove the filo dough from the freezer and set aside to thaw while preparing the filling. Heat the oil in a small skillet and sauté the garlic and leek for 5 minutes, or until the leek is soft. Add the spinach, mint, and cumin and stir-fry for 2 minutes, until the spinach begins to wilt. Remove from the heat and let cool.

Beat the feta cheese, ricotta, walnuts, lemon zest, and lemon juice together and stir into the spinach mixture.

Preheat the oven to 375°F. and lightly oil a large baking sheet.

Cut the pastry into 12 strips, 3½ × 18 inches. Melt the butter in a small saucepan and—keeping the remaining strips covered—brush one strip of pastry with the butter. Place a heaping tablespoon of filling at one end of the strip and fold over, diagonally from one side to the other, the length of the pastry to enclose the filling completely. Repeat to make 12 triangles.

Transfer the triangles to the prepared baking sheet and brush with the remaining butter. Bake for 25 minutes, or until the triangles are golden. Remove from the oven and let cool slightly.

continued

Strawberry and Olive Salad

Ingredients

12 large strawberries, hulled and sliced | 2 teaspoons extra-virgin olive oil
12 pitted black olives | 1 teaspoon balsamic vinegar
2 teaspoons minced fresh lemon balm (*optional*) | Salt and freshly ground black pepper

Toss the strawberries, olives, lemon balm,
olive oil, vinegar, and salt and pepper together
and arrange on serving plates, with 2 triangles
per person.

Broiled Tomato Toasts

SERVES 6 – 8

*Almost everywhere you go in Italy, you are served country bread rubbed with garlic and
drizzled with delicious olive oil. I like to add chopped tomatoes to the bread and broil it quickly
before serving. This is a good alternative to traditional garlic bread.*

Ingredients

2 large, ripe tomatoes, peeled, seeded, and chopped | ½ teaspoon lemon juice
1 large clove garlic, crushed | Pinch of sugar
2 tablespoons olive oil | Salt and freshly ground black pepper
1 tablespoon chopped fresh basil | 1 small baguette

Mix the tomatoes with the garlic, olive oil,
basil, lemon juice, sugar, and salt and pepper to
taste, and marinate for 1 hour.

Preheat the broiler.

Slice the baguette in half lengthwise and brown
lightly on both sides. Spread the tomato
mixture over the toast and return to the broiler
for 3 to 4 minutes, until hot.

Cut into bite-size pieces and serve at once.

Celeriac–White Stilton Mousse with Tomato Sauce

SERVES 6

Light and creamy, these mousses make an elegant appetizer for a dinner party. White Stilton cheese, which is milder than regular blue-veined Stilton, enhances the flavor of the celeriac without overpowering it. If you can't find white Stilton, try a tangy goat cheese.

Ingredients

MOUSSE	SAUCE
12 ounces celeriac (celery root), peeled and chopped	2 tablespoons olive oil
2 tablespoons (¼ stick) butter	2 shallots, finely chopped
2 ounces white Stilton, crumbled	1 clove garlic, crushed
½ cup fresh white bread crumbs	2 large, ripe tomatoes, chopped
4 tablespoons heavy cream	3 tablespoons dry white wine
1 egg, lightly beaten	1 tablespoon chopped fresh basil
	Pinch of sugar
	Salt and freshly ground white pepper

Preheat the oven to 350°F. Lightly oil and then line the bottoms of six ⅓-cup ramekins or custard cups with wax paper or parchment.

Steam the celeriac for 15 to 20 minutes, or until tender, then puree with the butter, cheese, and bread crumbs until smooth. Beat in the cream and egg. Spoon the mixture into the prepared dishes and place in a roasting pan. Pour in boiling water to come two-thirds of the way up the sides of the dishes. Bake for 15 to 20 minutes, or until firm to the touch. Remove from the oven and let rest for 5 minutes.

Meanwhile, heat the oil in a small skillet and sauté the shallots and garlic for 5 minutes, or until soft. Add the tomatoes, wine, basil, sugar, and salt and pepper. Cover and simmer over low heat for 15 minutes. Puree the sauce and pass it through a fine sieve.

Coat each serving plate with a little sauce, then unmold a mousse onto the center of each one. Serve immediately.

Baked Cheese with Figs and Arugula

SERVES 4

Baked in small ramekins, these cheese mousses are cut open to reveal a filling of tangy fig relish. The pleasantly bitter flavor of the arugula sets off the richness of the cheese.

Preheat the oven to 350°F. and lightly oil and line the bottoms of four ⅓-cup ramekins or custard cups with wax paper or parchment.

Melt the butter in a small saucepan and sauté the chopped figs for 2 minutes. Stir in the vinegar and sugar, cover, and simmer gently over very low heat for 2 minutes. Remove from the heat and let cool.

To make the mousse, cream the ricotta with the Parmesan, egg, and nutmeg. Fill each ramekin two-thirds full with the cheese mixture. Make a small well in the center of each cheese portion and spoon one-fourth of the fig relish into the wells.

Ingredients

FILLING
1 tablespoon butter
2 small fresh figs, finely chopped
1 teaspoon balsamic vinegar
½ teaspoon sugar

MOUSSE
1 cup (8 ounces) ricotta
¼ cup freshly grated Parmesan cheese
1 egg
Pinch of freshly grated nutmeg

SALAD
Small bunch of arugula
2 small fresh figs, thinly sliced
1 tablespoon olive oil
1 teaspoon balsamic vinegar
Salt and freshly ground black pepper

Top with the remaining cheese mixture and smooth the surface.

Place the ramekins in a roasting pan and pour in boiling water to come two-thirds of the way up the sides of the dishes. Place in the oven and bake for 18 to 20 minutes, or until the mousses are firm to the touch. Remove from the oven and let rest for 5 minutes.

Unmold the mousses onto serving plates and arrange the arugula and sliced figs around the edge. Blend the oil, vinegar, and seasonings and drizzle over the salad. Serve warm.

Parsnip and Gorgonzola Dolce Soufflés

*This simple but exquisite soufflé melts in your mouth. The subtle flavors of the parsnip, hazelnut,
and Gorgonzola dolce cheese combine to make this the most delicious soufflé I have tasted.
Do not worry if the soufflés sink—they invariably do, because it is their nature.
What's a little sunken soufflé among friends?*

Ingredients

3 tablespoons butter	1 medium parsnip, cooked and mashed
3 tablespoons all-purpose flour	Pinch of ground allspice
1 cup milk	Salt and freshly ground white pepper
¾ cup (3 ounces) crumbled Gorgonzola dolce (*dolcelatte*) cheese	⅓ cup hazelnuts, toasted and finely ground
3 eggs, separated	

Preheat the oven to 375°F. and lightly oil six
½-cup ramekins.

Melt the butter in a small saucepan and stir in
the flour. Cook for 1 minute and then gradually
add the milk, stirring until it thickens. Cook
for 2 minutes and allow to cool slightly.

Beat in the cheese, egg yolks, and mashed
parsnip, then stir in the allspice and salt
and pepper.

Whisk the egg whites until stiff and carefully
fold into the mixture along with half of the
hazelnuts. Sprinkle the remaining hazelnuts
into the prepared ramekins to coat the base
and sides. Spoon in the soufflé mixture and
place in a roasting pan. Pour in boiling water
to two-thirds of the way up the sides of the
dishes and bake for 30 to 35 minutes, until risen
and golden.

Remove from oven and serve immediately.

Zucchini Tartlets

SERVES 8

*The combination of dill and zucchini works well together in these creamy flans,
made in individual tartlet tins. Serve hot, warm, or cold with Tubbs's Tomato Salad (page 94).*

Sift the flour and salt together into a bowl and rub in the butter until the mixture resembles fine bread crumbs. Work in the egg yolk and 1 tablespoon water to form a soft dough. Add the remaining water if the dough is too firm. Cover with plastic wrap and refrigerate for 30 minutes.

Steam the zucchini whole for 10 to 15 minutes, or until just tender. Rinse under cold water to stop the cooking and pat dry. Cut into thin slices and set aside.

Remove the dough from the refrigerator and divide into 8 equal pieces. Roll out into thin circles about 5 inches across and use to line eight 4-inch tartlet tins. Prick the bases and chill for 15 minutes.

Preheat the oven to 425°F.

Line the pastry cases with aluminum foil and baking beans and bake "blind" for 8 minutes. Remove the foil and beans and bake for a further 5 to 7 minutes, or until the cases are lightly golden and crisp. Remove from the oven and let cool. Reduce the oven temperature to 375°F.

Melt the butter in a small skillet and sauté the scallions, garlic, and dill for 5 minutes. Cool slightly and spread over the pastry cases. Arrange the zucchini slices attractively over the top. Beat together the cream, eggs, mustard, and salt and pepper until combined and pour over the filling, being careful not to spill any over the sides of the pastry. Sprinkle with the cheese and bake for 20 to 25 minutes, or until risen and golden.

Remove from the oven and serve hot, or let cool on a wire rack.

Ingredients

PASTRY
1¼ cups all-purpose flour
½ teaspoon salt
7 tablespoons unsalted butter
1 egg yolk
1 to 2 teaspoons cold water

FILLING
2 medium zucchini
2 tablespoons (¼ stick) butter
8 scallions,
trimmed and finely chopped
1 clove garlic, crushed
1 tablespoon chopped fresh dill
½ cup half-and-half
2 small eggs, lightly beaten
2 tablespoons coarse grain mustard
Salt and freshly ground black pepper
2 ounces Gruyère cheese,
finely grated

Asparagus with Raspberry Hollandaise

SERVES 4

This is a delicious and unusual hollandaise sauce that I discovered by accident when I found only raspberry vinegar left in my kitchen cupboard. I have since refined the sauce by infusing fresh raspberries and reducing the resulting vinegar to a thick glossy liquid.

Place the vinegar and raspberries in a small bowl and set aside to infuse for 1 hour. Strain the liquid into a small, nonreactive saucepan and add the bay leaf and peppercorns. Bring to a boil and reduce until only 2 tablespoons of liquid remain. (This will only take a minute or so.) Strain into a heatproof bowl and cool slightly.

Beat in the egg yolks until pale and creamy, then place the bowl over a pan of gently simmering water. Drop in the butter, a little at a time, whisking well after each addition. Season with salt and pepper and keep warm.

Ingredients

HOLLANDAISE SAUCE
½ cup raspberry vinegar
¼ cup fresh raspberries
1 bay leaf
6 white peppercorns
2 egg yolks, at room temperature
8 tablespoons (1 stick) unsalted butter, softened and diced
Salt and freshly ground white pepper

1½ pounds fresh asparagus, trimmed

(*Note:* The sauce will curdle if the butter is added too quickly.)

Steam the asparagus for 8 to 10 minutes, depending on its size, until tender. Serve immediately with a spoonful of hollandaise poured over each portion.

Note: Hollandaise sauce can be made with success in a food processor. Strain the reduced vinegar mixture into the processor, add the egg yolks, and blend until creamy. Melt the butter and—with the motor running —pour the butter through the funnel in a gentle stream until the sauce is thickened.

Chilled Carrot-Ginger Mousse with Cucumber-Dill Salad

SERVES 6

Ingredients

MOUSSE	SALAD
1 pound carrots, roughly chopped	½ small cucumber, peeled
2 tablespoons (¼ stick) butter	1 teaspoon salt
1 small onion, finely chopped	2 tablespoons olive oil
2 teaspoons grated fresh ginger	2 teaspoons lemon juice
½ cup half-and-half	1 tablespoon chopped fresh dill
2 eggs	½ teaspoon honey
	Salt and freshly ground white pepper
	Dill sprigs, for garnish

Preheat the oven to 375°F. Lightly oil and line the bottoms of six ½-cup ramekins or custard cups with wax paper or parchment.

Steam the carrots for 15 minutes, or until tender. Melt the butter in a skillet and sauté the onion and ginger for 10 minutes. Stir in the carrots and continue to sauté for 5 minutes more. Puree until smooth, then cool slightly. Beat in the half-and-half and eggs, and spoon into the prepared ramekins. Place in a roasting pan and pour in boiling water to come two-thirds of the way up the sides of the dishes. Bake for 30 minutes, or until firm to the touch. Remove from the oven, let cool completely, then refrigerate for 1 hour.

Meanwhile, cut the cucumber in half lengthwise and scoop out the seeds. Sprinkle with the salt, place in a colander, and let drain for 30 minutes. Wash well, pat dry, then cut into thin slices and place in a bowl. Combine the olive oil, lemon juice, dill, honey, and salt and pepper to taste and toss with the cucumber. Refrigerate for 1 hour.

To serve, turn the mousses out onto serving plates and spoon the salad around them. Garnish with dill sprigs.

Herb and Saffron Ravioli

SERVES 6

I find kneading dough by hand to be therapeutic, so I roll pasta dough by hand instead of using a pasta machine. When you are next in need of therapy, try these tasty herb ravioli filled with sun-dried tomatoes and ricotta, and tossed in a light saffron butter. They make an elegant first course for a dinner party.

Ingredients

PASTA
1½ cups all-purpose flour
1 teaspoon salt
¼ cup basil leaves, finely chopped
2 large eggs and 1 large egg yolk, lightly beaten
A little olive oil

FILLING
2 tablespoons (¼ stick) butter
2 small shallots, finely chopped
1 clove garlic, finely chopped
¼ cup sun-dried tomatoes packed in oil, drained and chopped
1 cup (8 ounces) crumbled ricotta

¼ cup grated Parmesan cheese
2 tablespoons pine nuts, toasted (*page 8*)
Pinch of freshly grated nutmeg
Salt and freshly ground white pepper

SAUCE
8 tablespoons (1 stick) unsalted butter, softened
Large pinch of saffron strands
1 clove garlic, crushed
Salt and freshly ground black pepper

Flour for dusting

Sift the flour and salt into a large bowl and stir in the basil. Make a well in the center and work in the eggs and egg yolk and a drizzle of oil to form a soft, pliable dough. Knead for 5 minutes, or until the dough is smooth and elastic. Cover and let the dough rest for 30 minutes.

Melt the butter in a small skillet and sauté the shallots and garlic for 5 minutes, or until the shallots are soft. Stir in the tomatoes and remove from the heat. Let cool slightly, then mix in the ricotta, Parmesan, pine nuts, and nutmeg. Season and set aside.

Blend the butter, saffron, garlic, and salt and pepper in a bowl until combined and set aside.

When the dough is rested, divide in half. On a lightly floured surface, roll one half of the dough out into a 12 × 10-inch rectangle and place 30 teaspoons of filling at 2½-inch intervals over it. With a moistened pastry brush, dampen the dough around the filling. Roll out the remaining dough and place the second sheet over the first, pressing down between the mounds of filling to seal. Using a 2½-inch fluted pastry cutter, cut apart the ravioli and leave them to dry slightly on a wire rack.

Bring a large saucepan of water to a boil and drop in the ravioli in batches. Cook for 4 to 5 minutes, or until the parcels are cooked through. Remove with a slotted spoon and keep warm. Repeat with the remaining ravioli.

Quickly melt the prepared sauce in a small saucepan and pour over the ravioli. Serve immediately.

Note: The pasta dough can be made in a food processor. Place all the ingredients in the bowl and process until the mixture forms a smooth, firm dough. Cover and let rest.

If using a pasta machine, make the dough as above and let it rest. Set the pasta machine rollers to the widest setting. Cut the dough into small pieces, flatten slightly, and pass each piece through the pasta machine. Repeat once and reduce setting on machine. Pass the dough through each setting twice. Continue this process, each time reducing the setting on the pasta machine, to form long thin sheets of pasta dough, similar to lasagne. The dough is then ready to be filled and shaped, as above.

Salad of Broiled Tomatoes and Mozzarella

Mozzarella originated in southern Italy, where it is still made from water-buffalo milk.
If possible, buy buffalo mozzarella for this recipe because it is softer and creamier than cows'
milk mozzarella. This is particularly important when the mozzarella is served raw.

Ingredients

3 large, ripe tomatoes	Pinch of sugar
2 tablespoons olive paste	Salt and freshly ground black pepper
6 ounces *mozzarella de bufala*	1 tablespoon chopped fresh basil
3 tablespoons extra-virgin olive oil	1 tablespoon pine nuts, toasted
2 teaspoons balsamic vinegar	(*page 8*)
1 teaspoon Dijon mustard	Salad greens, as desired

Preheat the broiler.

Cut the tomatoes into quarters and scoop out and discard the seeds. Spread each quarter with a little olive paste.

Broil the tomatoes for 3 to 4 minutes, or until just soft. Transfer to a plate and set aside to cool completely.

When ready to serve, thinly slice the mozzarella and arrange it on serving plates with the tomatoes.

Blend the olive oil, vinegar, mustard, sugar, and salt and pepper and drizzle over the mozzarella. Sprinkle the basil and nuts over the dressing and serve with a garnish of salad greens.

28

Soups

Red Pepper Soup with Cheese and Herb Floats

The peppers are broiled before being pureed for this soup, which gives them an intense smoky flavor that enhances the richness of the soup. A mixture of cheese, egg, and herbs is shaped into ovals and poached lightly. The ovals are "floated" on the soup before serving. The recipe is finished with a generous grinding of black pepper.

Ingredients

4 medium red bell peppers
3 tablespoons olive oil
1 clove garlic
1 red onion, sliced
1 medium potato, peeled and diced
1 tablespoon chopped fresh parsley
1 teaspoon chopped fresh sage
3⅓ cups water

½ cup tomato juice
1 tablespoon balsamic vinegar
Pinch of cayenne pepper
Cheese and Herb Floats
  (recipe follows)

½ cup half-and-half
Basil sprigs, for garnish

Preheat the broiler and place the peppers under it. Broil for 10 to 15 minutes, turning the peppers from time to time, until they are charred on all sides. Place in a plastic bag and leave for 30 minutes, until cool enough to handle.

Heat the oil in a 3-quart saucepan and sauté the garlic and onion for 5 minutes. Add the potato, parsley, and sage, and sauté for a further 2 minutes. Add the water, tomato juice, vinegar, and cayenne. Bring to a boil, cover, and simmer over low heat for 20 minutes.

Remove the peppers from the bag. Peel and discard the skins and seeds, reserving any juices. Place the peppers, juices, and the soup in a blender and puree until very smooth. Return to the pan, stir in the cream, and heat through without boiling.

Spoon the soup into bowls, top each one with 2 or 3 Cheese and Herb Floats, and garnish with basil sprigs. Serve at once with Seeded Cornmeal Soda Rolls *(page 116)*.

Cheese and Herb Floats

Ingredients

½ cup (4 ounces) ricotta
3 tablespoons finely grated pecorino cheese
1 egg, lightly beaten
2 tablespoons fine semolina

2 tablespoons chopped fresh mixed herbs (basil, tarragon, thyme, sage)
Pinch of freshly grated nutmeg
Squeeze of lemon juice
Salt and freshly ground black pepper

Place the ricotta, pecorino, egg, semolina, herbs, nutmeg, and lemon juice in a bowl and beat until smooth. Season with salt and pepper. Cover and refrigerate for 10 minutes to firm up.

Bring a large skillet of water to a steady simmer. Shape the cheese mixture into ovals by using 2 small teaspoons to pass a spoonful of the mixture from one spoon to the other until you have an egg shape. Drop the ovals into the simmering water in batches and poach for 3 to 4 minutes, or until they rise to the surface and are firm to the touch. Remove with a slotted spoon and drain on absorbent paper.

Mixed Vegetable Soup with Fresh Coriander Pistou

SERVES 6

I discovered the delights of pistou only recently, thanks to a friend who had just returned from Provence. This versatile sauce is a blend of basil, garlic, olive oil, Parmesan cheese, and sometimes pine nuts. It is pounded—hence the French name pistou—and stirred into soups and pasta dishes. For a Middle Eastern flavor, I have substituted coriander for the basil and cashews for the pine nuts. It makes a delicious, hearty soup.

Ingredients

STOCK
¾ cup (6 ounces) dried chick-peas (garbanzo beans), soaked overnight
3¾ cups cold water
1 3-inch celery stalk
1 clove garlic

2 sprigs of thyme
4 sprigs of fresh coriander (cilantro)
¼ teaspoon cumin seeds
¼ teaspoon fennel seeds

continued

SOUP	
2 tablespoons olive oil	1 medium potato, diced
1 clove garlic, finely minced	1 cup green beans, trimmed and
1 teaspoon grated fresh ginger	cut into short lengths
1 medium leek, trimmed and thinly sliced	1 cup shelled fresh fava beans
2 celery stalks, sliced	2 medium zucchini, sliced
	Salt and freshly ground black pepper

Drain the soaked chick-peas, place in a 3-quart saucepan, and add the water. Tie the celery, garlic, thyme, coriander, cumin, and fennel in a small piece of cheesecloth and add to the pan. Bring to a boil; cook over high heat for 10 minutes, then reduce the heat, cover, and simmer gently for 50 to 60 minutes, or until the chick-peas are tender.

Meanwhile, heat the oil in a large skillet and sauté the garlic, ginger, leek, and celery for 5 minutes. Add the potato and stir-fry for 2 to 3 minutes, then set aside.

Drain the cooked chick-peas and reserve. Add enough water to make 3 cups of stock, if necessary. Return the stock to the pan and add the sautéed vegetables, chick-peas, green beans, fava beans, and zucchini. Bring to a boil, cover, and simmer gently over low heat for 10 to 15 minutes, or until the vegetables are tender. Season to taste with salt and pepper and keep warm.

Pistou

Ingredients

PISTOU	
2 cloves garlic, minced	2 tablespoons olive oil
½ cup fresh coriander (cilantro) leaves	2 tablespoons freshly grated
¼ cup cashew nuts, toasted	Parmesan cheese
	Salt and freshly ground black pepper

For the pistou, blend or grind the garlic, coriander, and cashew nuts to a fairly smooth paste. Gradually stir in the olive oil and cheese, and season with salt and pepper.

Heat the soup through and serve with a generous spoonful of the pistou with each serving.

Chick-Pea and Spinach Soup with Nutmeg

SERVES 6

*I am a great lover of nutmeg. Here it is grated into the soup as it is served,
becoming the predominant flavor.*

Ingredients

STOCK	SOUP
1 cup (8 ounces) dried chick-peas (garbanzo beans), soaked overnight	2 tablespoons (¼ stick) butter
5 cups water	1 medium onion, chopped
1 small onion, chopped	1 clove garlic, crushed
1 clove garlic, peeled	½ pound spinach leaves, thinly shredded
1 3-inch celery stalk	2 tablespoons chopped fresh parsley
1 bay leaf	3 tablespoons tomato paste
2 sprigs of thyme	1 tablespoon lemon juice
6 black peppercorns	Salt and freshly ground black pepper
½ cup (4 ounces) green lentils, washed	
	6 to 8 tablespoons freshly grated Parmesan cheese
	1 whole nutmeg

Drain the soaked chick-peas, place in a 3-quart saucepan, and cover with water. Tie the onion, garlic, celery, bay leaf, thyme, and peppercorns in a small piece of cheesecloth, and add to the pan. Bring to a boil and cook over high heat for 10 minutes, then reduce the heat, cover, and simmer gently for 50 minutes. Add the lentils and continue to simmer for another 20 to 30 minutes, until the chick-peas and lentils are tender.

Strain the liquid into a measuring cup, reserving the chick-peas and lentils, and add enough water to make 5 cups, if necessary. Discard the cheesecloth bag.

Melt the butter in a clean saucepan and sauté the onion and garlic for 5 minutes. Stir in the spinach and parsley, and sauté over low heat for 2 to 3 minutes. Add the reserved stock, chick-peas, lentils, tomato paste, lemon juice, and salt and pepper. Bring to a boil and simmer for 5 minutes.

Serve the soup sprinkled with Parmesan and freshly grated nutmeg.

Broccoli and Almond Soup with Lemon Butter

This is one of my favorite winter soups. The almonds are toasted and ground, providing a rich, nutty flavor that is set off by the piquancy of the lemon butter.

Ingredients

SOUP	LEMON BUTTER
1 tablespoon olive oil	8 tablespoons (1 stick) unsalted butter, softened
2 medium leeks, trimmed and thinly sliced	2 teaspoons grated lemon zest
1 pound broccoli, coarsely chopped	2 teaspoons lemon juice
1 medium potato, coarsely chopped	Salt and freshly ground black pepper
¾ cup blanched almonds, toasted and finely ground	1 tablespoon lemon juice
1 teaspoon chopped fresh thyme	
1 bay leaf	
5½ cups Vegetable Stock (page 45)	

Heat the oil in a 2-quart saucepan and sauté the leeks for 5 minutes, until soft. Add the broccoli and potato and sauté for a further 5 minutes.

Stir in the almonds, thyme, bay leaf, and stock. Bring to a boil, cover, and simmer gently for 20 to 25 minutes.

Meanwhile, cream the butter, lemon zest, lemon juice, and salt and pepper. Form into a log and wrap in aluminum foil. Refrigerate for 20 minutes.

Remove the bay leaf and puree the soup in a blender until smooth. Return to the pan, season, and stir in 1 tablespoon lemon juice. Heat through.

Remove the lemon butter from the refrigerator and cut into 12 slices. Pour the soup into serving bowls and top each with 2 slices of lemon butter. Serve with crusty whole wheat bread.

Miff's Spicy Pumpkin Soup

SERVES 4 – 6

This soup brings back memories—not of Halloween, but of Guy Fawkes night. Every November 5, my Aunt Miff would hold a fireworks party, and all the children would spend hours preparing pumpkin lanterns to hang in the garden. We would watch the fireworks, huddled around the bonfire, with mugs of steaming pumpkin soup.

Ingredients

1 tablespoon olive oil
4 shallots, chopped
2 celery stalks, sliced
2 medium carrots, coarsely chopped
2 medium potatoes, diced
1 tablespoon ground coriander
2 teaspoons ground cumin
½ teaspoon ground cinnamon

¼ teaspoon ground cloves
Pinch of freshly grated nutmeg
2 pounds pumpkin, peeled, seeded, and coarsely chopped
5 cups Vegetable Stock (*page 45*)
Plain yogurt and fresh coriander (cilantro) leaves, for garnish

Heat the oil in a 3-quart saucepan and sauté the shallots and celery for 5 minutes. Add the carrots and potatoes and sauté for a further 5 minutes. Add the coriander, cumin, cinnamon, cloves, and nutmeg, and stir-fry for 2 minutes. Add the pumpkin and stock, bring to a boil, cover, and simmer gently for 20 minutes, or until all the vegetables are tender.

Blend the soup in a food processor or blender until smooth and return to the pan. Adjust the seasonings and heat through.

Serve hot, garnished with a swirl of yogurt and some coriander leaves.

Bean and Buckwheat Broth

Roasted buckwheat, also called kasha, is available at good health food stores and supermarkets.
Alternatively, you can roast your own. Stir-fry buckwheat in a skillet over high heat for
2 to 3 minutes, until it is golden and gives off a slightly smoky aroma.
Remove from the heat and allow to cool.

Ingredients

STOCK	SOUP
1¾ cups borlotti beans, pinto beans, or red kidney beans, soaked overnight	¾ cup roasted buckwheat (kasha)
1 quart water	1 tablespoon olive oil
1 3-inch celery stalk	2 medium onions, finely chopped
1 bay leaf	2 medium carrots, finely chopped
1 clove garlic, peeled but left whole	4 ripe tomatoes, peeled, seeded, and chopped
6 white peppercorns	1 tablespoon capers
2 sprigs of parsley	2 teaspoons Worcestershire sauce
2 sprigs of basil	2 tablespoons chopped fresh parsley
	1 tablespoon chopped fresh basil
	Salt and freshly ground black pepper
	Bread and garlic to serve

Drain the beans and place in a 3-quart saucepan. Add the water and bring to a boil. Tie the celery, bay leaf, garlic, peppercorns, parsley, and basil in a square of cheesecloth and add to the saucepan. Cook over high heat for 10 minutes, then lower the heat, cover, and simmer gently for 45 to 50 minutes, or until the beans are tender.

Soak the buckwheat in plenty of water for 10 minutes, then drain. Heat the oil in a clean saucepan and sauté the onions and carrots for 10 minutes, until lightly browned.

Strain the cooked beans, discarding the cheesecloth bag and reserving the stock and beans. Add enough water to make 4 cups of stock, if necessary. Add the tomatoes, capers, Worcestershire sauce, parsley, and basil to the pan with the beans. Bring to a boil, cover, and simmer gently for 20 minutes.

Season to taste with salt and pepper and serve the soup hot, with toasted bread rubbed with garlic.

Tomato, Apple, and Celery Soup

SERVES 4

I first tasted this soup, or a similar one, at a friend's house. It was served hot and was delicious. I have adapted it by serving it chilled and adding fresh mint. Try it either way—both are wonderfully refreshing.

Ingredients

2 tablespoons olive oil	2½ cups water
1 small red onion, finely chopped	1 tablespoon lemon juice
4 celery stalks, finely chopped	1 tablespoon sugar
1 clove garlic, crushed	1 tablespoon chopped fresh mint
2 pounds ripe tomatoes, peeled, seeded, and chopped	½ cup half-and-half
⅓ cup dry white wine	Salt and freshly ground black pepper
2 tart, ripe apples, peeled, cored, and coarsely chopped	

Heat the oil in a 2-quart saucepan and sauté the onion, celery, and garlic for 5 minutes. Stir in the tomatoes and wine, bring to a boil, and simmer rapidly for 5 minutes.

Add the apples, water, lemon juice, sugar, and mint; bring to a boil, cover, and simmer over low heat for 20 minutes.

Puree the soup until very smooth. Pass through a fine sieve and set aside until completely cool.

Refrigerate the soup for at least an hour before serving. Stir in the half-and-half until combined, season to taste, and serve with Walnut and Poppy Seed Loaf *(page 117)*.

N o t e : Use yogurt cheese *(page 8)* or crème fraîche instead of half-and-half, if preferred.

Greenhill Pea and Leek Soup

SERVES 4

I had the good fortune of growing up on a farm, where my father grew acres of fresh peas.
I have vivid memories of sitting among baskets of those peas, consuming as many as I could before
they were packed off to the market. This fresh-tasting minted pea soup is an old favorite.

Ingredients

1 tablespoon olive oil
4 young leeks, trimmed and sliced
4 scallions, trimmed and chopped
1 clove garlic, crushed
2 cups shelled fresh peas
2 tablespoons chopped fresh mint

4 cups Vegetable Stock *(page 45)*
Salt and freshly ground black pepper

Plain yogurt and fresh mint,
for garnish

Heat the oil in a 2-quart saucepan and sauté the leeks, scallions, and garlic for 10 minutes, or until the leeks are soft.

Add the peas, mint, and stock and season with salt and pepper. Bring to a boil, cover, and simmer gently for 20 minutes, until the peas are tender.

Puree the soup until smooth, season to taste, and garnish with a swirl of yogurt and fresh mint.

Curried Parsnip and Coconut Soup with Pear Coulis

Spicy Indian dishes are frequently accompanied by sweet relishes and chutneys. Here a highly spiced soup is served with a sweet fruit puree—a classic example of the successful balance between sweet and savory.

Ingredients

SOUP
2 tablespoons (¼ stick) butter
1 medium onion, chopped
1 clove garlic, crushed
2 teaspoons grated fresh ginger
1 pound parsnips, coarsely chopped
2 medium carrots, coarsely chopped
1 tablespoon curry powder
½ teaspoon ground turmeric
½ teaspoon ground cinnamon
3⅓ cups Vegetable Stock *(page 45)*

2 bay leaves
1 teaspoon salt

COULIS
1 tablespoon butter
1 large pear, peeled, cored, and finely chopped
1 tablespoon sugar
Juice of ½ lemon

¼ cup unsweetened coconut milk
½ cup boiling water

Melt the butter in a 3-quart saucepan and sauté the onion, garlic, and ginger for 5 minutes. Stir in the parsnips and carrots and continue to sauté for a further 5 minutes. Add the curry powder, turmeric, and cinnamon and stir-fry for 2 minutes. Add the stock, bay leaves, and salt; bring to a boil, cover, and simmer over low heat for 25 minutes, or until all the vegetables are tender. Set aside to cool slightly, remove bay leaf, and blend until smooth.

Melt the butter for the coulis in a small saucepan and sauté the pear for 5 minutes, or until soft. Add the sugar and lemon juice, and stir until the sugar is dissolved. Puree the sauce and keep warm.

Blend the coconut milk with the boiling water until smooth, and stir into the soup. Return the soup to the pan and heat through, without boiling, for about 5 minutes. Serve the soup hot with a swirl of pear coulis in each bowl.

SOUPS

44

Vegetable Stock

I make up many different stocks, depending on the dish I am preparing. Here is a versatile stock that adds depth and body to a dish. I use it frequently for many soups and sauces. Strain the stock immediately to avoid any bitterness the herbs and vegetables may retain, which could spoil it.

Ingredients

4 tablespoons olive oil	⅔ cup red lentils
2 cloves garlic, minced	6 sprigs of parsley
2 medium onions, sliced	4 sprigs of thyme
2 large leeks, trimmed and sliced	4 sprigs of basil
4 medium carrots, chopped	4 bay leaves
2 medium potatoes, chopped	2 quarts water
6 celery stalks, sliced	2 teaspoons salt
8 ripe tomatoes, quartered	12 black peppercorns
½ pound mushrooms, wiped and quartered	

Heat the oil in a 3-quart saucepan and sauté the garlic, onions, and leeks for 10 minutes, until browned. Add the carrots, potatoes, and celery and sauté for 10 minutes more.

Add the tomatoes, mushrooms, lentils, parsley, thyme, basil, bay leaves, water, salt and peppercorns to the pan. Bring to a boil, cover, and simmer over low heat for 30 minutes.

Strain through a fine sieve, cool, and reserve the stock until required.

Note: This stock can be kept for several days in the refrigerator.

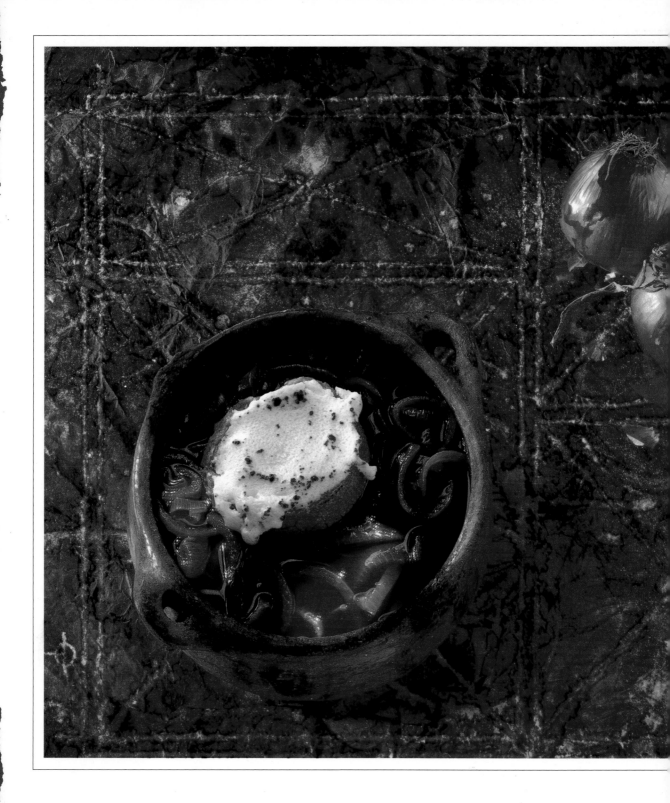

Red Onion Soup with Goat Cheese Toasts

SERVES 4

This is a variation on the classic French onion soup. The onions need to be sautéed for a very long time to allow their sweet flavor to develop and to become more digestible. For a refreshing change from the standard Gruyère, top the soup with goat cheese, which is spread over the bread and broiled.

Ingredients

SOUP
4 tablespoons (½ stick) butter
2 pounds red onions, thinly sliced
2 large cloves garlic, crushed
2 teaspoons chopped fresh thyme
1 teaspoon sugar
½ cup dry red wine
2 tablespoons port wine
3¾ cups Vegetable Stock *(page 45)*
Salt and freshly ground black pepper

TOPPING
8 ½-inch slices of French bread
2 ounces goat cheese

Melt the butter in a 2-quart sauce-pan and sauté the onions over medium heat for 25 to 30 minutes, or until well browned. Do not allow the onions to burn or they will become bitter.

Add the garlic, thyme, and sugar, and stir-fry for 2 minutes. Add the wines and cook over high heat to reduce the liquid to 4 tablespoons. Add the stock, bring to a boil, cover, and simmer over low heat for 20 minutes.

Season to taste with salt and pepper.

For the topping, preheat the broiler and toast the bread lightly on both sides. Cool slightly and spread one side of each toast with the goat cheese.

Pour the soup into heatproof bowls. Place 2 toasts in each bowl and broil for 2 to 3 minutes, until the cheese is bubbling and golden. Serve immediately.

Main Courses

Beet Tagliatelle with Shredded Spinach and Walnuts

SERVES 4

This fresh pasta is a very pretty shade of pink because it is colored with beet paste.
I find that its flavor combines well with the walnut oil and just-wilted spinach.
N o t e : Puree 1 large cooked beet in a food processor to make enough paste for this recipe.

Ingredients

PASTA
2 cups all-purpose flour
1 teaspoon salt
2 large eggs and 1 large yolk,
lightly beaten
3 tablespoons beet paste
A little oil

SAUCE
4 tablespoons walnut oil
2 cloves garlic, finely chopped
2 tablespoons chopped fresh basil
1 tablespoon grated lemon zest
8 ounces spinach leaves,
finely shredded
Pinch of freshly grated nutmeg
½ cup walnuts,
coarsely chopped and toasted
Salt and freshly ground black pepper

Basil leaves, for garnish

Sift the flour and salt into a large bowl. Make a well in the center and work in the eggs, egg yolk, beet paste, and a little oil to form a soft, pliable dough. Knead for 5 minutes, or until smooth and elastic. Cover and let rest for 30 minutes.

Divide the dough into 4 pieces and roll 1 piece to a rectangle ⅛ inch thick. Dust with flour and roll up loosely from one narrow end. With a sharp knife, cut the roll at ¼-inch intervals, to form the tagliatelle. Unfold loosely and let dry slightly on a floured towel. Repeat with the remaining pasta pieces.

Bring a large saucepan of salted water to a boil. At the same time, heat the walnut oil in a large skillet and sauté the garlic, basil, and lemon zest for 2 to 3 minutes.

Drop the tagliatelle into the boiling water, return to the boil, and simmer over medium heat for 2 to 3 minutes, until the pasta is *al dente*—just done.

Stir the spinach and nutmeg into the garlic and basil until the spinach just starts to wilt, and remove from the heat.

Drain the pasta and toss with the spinach. Serve immediately, sprinkled with walnuts, lots of salt and pepper, and basil leaves.

Leek and Ricotta Tart

SERVES 8

We have all heard people say, "It tastes almost as good as my mother's." Well, this recipe— with only a couple of small changes—is my mother's! I have added a little grated Parmesan to the pastry and topped the tart with black olives. My mother tested my version in a local cooking competition—it won her a gold star—so this tart comes highly recommended.

Ingredients

PASTRY
1¼ cups all-purpose flour
Pinch of salt
8 tablespoons (1 stick) unsalted butter
¼ cup freshly grated Parmesan cheese
1 egg yolk
2 to 3 tablespoons cold water

FILLING
2 tablespoons olive oil
1 pound young leeks, trimmed and thinly sliced
1 tablespoon chopped fresh sage
2 eggs
1 cup (8 ounces) ricotta
2 ounces Gruyère cheese, grated
½ cup heavy cream
Salt and freshly ground black pepper
¼ cup pitted black olives, halved

Make the pastry. Sift the flour and salt into a bowl and rub in the butter until the mixture resembles fine bread crumbs. Stir in the cheese and work in the egg yolk and 2 tablespoons water to form a smooth, soft dough. Add the extra tablespoon of water if the dough is too firm. Wrap and refrigerate for 30 minutes.

Preheat the oven to 400°F.

Make the filling. Heat the oil in a large skillet and sauté the leeks and sage for 10 minutes, or until the leeks are soft. Cool slightly.

Roll out the dough and line a 9- to 10-inch deep fluted tart pan. Prick the bottom to keep the pastry from puffing. Chill for 10 minutes.

Line the tart pastry with aluminum foil and fill with baking beans. Bake "blind" for 10 minutes, then remove the foil and beans and bake for 10 to 12 minutes more, or until the pastry is lightly golden and crisp. Remove from the oven and let cool. Reduce the temperature to 375°F.

Beat the eggs, ricotta, Gruyère, cream, and salt and pepper together. Spread the leeks over the tart base and pour in the cheese mixture. Sprinkle the olives on top of the cheese mixture and bake for 25 to 30 minutes, or until golden and firm to the touch.

Remove the tart from the oven and serve hot, warm, or cold, with a crisp green salad.

Tipsy Parsnips

SERVES 4–6

I love the combination of sweet and savory, and I particularly like this dish. The parsnips and onions are sautéed and served with apple slices in a glazed fruit sauce. I have used British hard cider for this recipe, but apple juice works equally well.

Ingredients

2 tablespoons (¼ stick) butter	2 teaspoons fennel seeds
2 McIntosh or Red Delicious apples, cored, quartered, and thickly sliced	1 tablespoon chopped fresh sage
1 tablespoon olive oil	1 cup hard cider or apple juice
1 clove garlic, crushed	1 cup Vegetable Stock *(page 45)*
12 ounces baby parsnips, halved	1 tablespoon whole-grain mustard
8 ounces pearl onions, halved	1 teaspoon honey
	Salt and freshly ground black pepper

Heat the butter in a large skillet over medium heat, and sauté the apples for 4 to 5 minutes, turning frequently, until golden on both sides. Remove from the heat and set aside.

Heat the oil in a clean skillet and sauté the garlic, parsnips, onions, and fennel seeds for 10 minutes, or until lightly browned. Add the sage, cider or apple juice, and stock; bring to a boil, cover, and simmer gently for 12 minutes.

Add the apples and their juices to the pan and simmer for 3 minutes more. Strain the juices into a small saucepan and keep the parsnip mixture warm in a serving dish. Stir the mustard and honey into the pan, bring to a boil, and simmer rapidly for 5 minutes, or until the liquid is reduced slightly and glossy. Pour over the vegetables, season to taste with salt and pepper, and serve at once.

Gnocchi with Pesto and Tomato-Gorgonzola Sauce

SERVES 4–6

Gnocchi, the Italian word for "dumplings," are wonderful to eat when you crave something comforting. They are shaped into little balls and boiled gently in water until they rise to the top. Everyone has his or her preferred recipe for a basic tomato sauce. Mine is simple. The long cooking time brings out the full flavor of the tomatoes, resulting in a deep, rich sauce. Try it with Gorgonzola cheese added at the last minute, served with the fresh gnocchi and pesto.

Ingredients

TOMATO-GORGONZOLA SAUCE

2 pounds (approximately 10 to 12 medium) ripe tomatoes

3 tablespoons extra-virgin olive oil

2 large cloves garlic, crushed

1 tablespoon chopped fresh basil

⅓ cup dry white wine

2 tablespoons tomato paste

2 bay leaves

Pinch of sugar

1 cup (4 ounces) crumbled Gorgonzola cheese

PESTO

1 clove garlic, chopped

¼ cup pine nuts

⅓ cup tightly packed basil leaves

⅓ cup extra-virgin olive oil

2 tablespoons freshly grated Parmesan cheese

Salt and freshly ground black pepper

GNOCCHI

1½ pounds potatoes, peeled

2 egg yolks

Salt and freshly ground black pepper

½ cup all-purpose flour

Put the tomatoes, olive oil, garlic, basil, wine, tomato paste, bay leaves, and sugar into a 2-quart saucepan. Bring to a boil, reduce the heat, and simmer gently, uncovered, for 1¼ to 1½ hours, until the sauce is thick. Puree and return to the pan.

Meanwhile, make the pesto. Blend together the garlic, pine nuts, and basil leaves to form a fairly smooth paste. Stir in the oil and Parmesan, and season to taste.

For the gnocchi, cook the potatoes in plenty of water until tender. Drain well to ensure the potatoes are dry and mash with the egg yolks and salt and pepper while still warm. Work in the flour to form a smooth, soft dough. Shape into small balls the size of large walnuts, and flatten slightly with a finger or the back of a fork.

Bring a 3-quart saucepan of water to a steady simmer and drop in the gnocchi, in batches. Simmer gently for 5 to 6 minutes, or until they rise to the surface and turn slightly opaque. Drain well and toss with 4 tablespoons of the pesto.

Reheat the tomato sauce quickly and stir in the cheese until combined. Serve immediately with the sauce poured over the gnocchi and extra pesto sauce passed separately, if desired.

Note: The remaining pesto can be stored in the refrigerator for up to 1 week, or frozen. It's a good idea to freeze lots of pesto when you have a large supply of fresh basil.

Saffron Risotto with Wild Mushrooms and Arugula

SERVES 4

Arugula is a peppery green that is stirred into this risotto at the last minute to add extra color and texture. Use a variety of wild or cultivated wild mushrooms, such as porcini or cèpes, oyster mushrooms, and shiitake.

Ingredients

2 cups Vegetable Stock (*page 45*)
Pinch of saffron strands
4 tablespoons (½ cup) butter
1 small onion, finely chopped
1 clove garlic, crushed
1¼ cups Arborio rice
½ cup dry white wine
2 tablespoons olive oil
1 cup (6 ounces) fresh wild mushrooms
1 cup (4 ounces) tightly packed arugula
½ cup freshly grated Parmesan or pecorino cheese
Salt and freshly ground black pepper

Heat the stock in a small saucepan, add the saffron, and let infuse for 10 minutes.

Heat the butter in a medium skillet and sauté the onion and garlic for 5 minutes, or until soft. Add the rice and stir over medium heat for 2 to 3 minutes, or until the rice is opaque. Pour in the wine and simmer rapidly until most of the liquid has evaporated. Add a third of the stock, stir once, and simmer gently over a low heat until the liquid is absorbed. Repeat this twice with the remaining stock, until the rice is tender, about 25 minutes.

Just before the rice is cooked, heat the oil in a small skillet and stir-fry the mushrooms over high heat until golden. Reduce the heat, add the arugula, and stir-fry for a few seconds, until just wilted.

Stir the mushrooms and arugula into the rice, along with the Parmesan, salt, and plenty of pepper. Serve immediately.

Vegetable Cassoulet

SERVES 6 – 8

The classic cassoulet—slowly cooked beans with different meats and sausages—is a specialty of Languedoc, the region of France that is just west of Provence. I have developed a vegetarian alternative, and it is delicious.

Ingredients

STOCK

1 cup dried white haricot beans, soaked overnight

3 cups water

1 3-inch celery stalk

2 sprigs thyme

2 sprigs rosemary

2 sprigs sage

1 bay leaf

6 black peppercorns

STEW

5 tablespoons olive oil

1 clove garlic, crushed

1 cup pearl onions, peeled

2 cups chopped carrots

1 fennel bulb, trimmed and finely chopped

3 cups chopped fresh mushrooms

1 medium eggplant, coarsely chopped

2 ripe tomatoes, peeled, seeded, and chopped

1 tablespoon chopped fresh thyme

1 tablespoon chopped fresh rosemary

½ cup dry white wine

½ cup tomato juice

⅓ cup red lentils

TOPPING

1 cup freshly grated Parmesan cheese

1 cup fresh whole wheat bread crumbs

Drain the soaked beans, place in a 3-quart saucepan, and pour in the water. Tie the celery, thyme, rosemary, sage, bay leaf, and peppercorns in a small piece of cheesecloth and add to the pan. Bring to a boil and cook over high heat for 10 minutes, then reduce the heat, cover, and simmer gently for 45 to 50 minutes, until the beans are tender.

Discard the cheesecloth bag, reserve the beans, and strain the stock into a clean saucepan. Bring to a boil and reduce to 1½ cups. Reserve.

Preheat the oven to 375°F. Lightly oil a shallow ovenproof dish with a 2-quart capacity.

For the stew, heat 2 tablespoons of the oil in a large skillet and sauté the garlic, onions, carrots, and fennel for 10 minutes, or until lightly browned. Remove with a slotted spoon and drain on paper towels. Add the remaining oil to the pan and stir-fry the mushrooms, eggplant, tomatoes, thyme, and rosemary for 5 minutes. Return the onion mixture to the pan, add the wine, and cook over high heat until most of the liquid is evaporated. Stir in the tomato juice, lentils, and reserved stock and simmer, uncovered, over a low heat for 15 minutes. Add the reserved beans, cover, and simmer gently for 10 minutes more.

Spoon the stew into the prepared dish, sprinkle the cheese and bread crumbs on top, and bake for 30 minutes, until bubbling and golden. Serve hot.

Spiced Vegetable Pakoras with Mango Relish

SERVES 4–6

Pakoras *are deep-fried, batter-dipped fritters, and eating them is a national pastime throughout India. You can use almost any vegetable in addition to the four I suggest here. The batter should be the consistency of heavy cream, so add the water gradually until you achieve this texture. Serve the pakoras with this tangy mango relish, which is quick and easy to prepare. It can be made in advance and stored in the refrigerator until required.*

Ingredients

VEGETABLES	BATTER
1 small eggplant, cut into ¼-inch slices	1⅓ cups chick-pea or all-purpose flour
1 teaspoon salt	1 tablespoon chopped fresh coriander (cilantro)
2 medium zucchini, cut into 1-inch slices	1 teaspoon salt
12 cauliflower florets	2 teaspoons curry powder
6 large button mushrooms, wiped and cut in half	1 tablespoon olive oil
	1 tablespoon lemon juice
	¾ to 1 cup ice water

Vegetable oil, for deep-frying

Lemon wedges and coriander or parsley, for garnish

Place the eggplant in a colander, sprinkle with the salt, and let drain while preparing the other vegetables.

Blanch the zucchini and cauliflower florets separately for 2 minutes in boiling water. Drain, refresh under cold water, and dry well. Rinse the eggplant and pat dry.

Combine the flour, coriander, salt, and curry powder in a large bowl. Gradually beat in the oil, lemon juice, and water until the batter is the consistency of heavy cream. Alternatively, place all the ingredients—except the water—in a food processor, and with the motor running, pour the water through the funnel until you have the right consistency.

continued

Heat 4 inches of oil in a deep, heavy-bottomed saucepan to 350°F.

Lightly whisk the batter and dip the vegetables in batches of 5 to 6, then slip them carefully into the hot oil. Fry the pakoras for 2 to 3 minutes on each side, turning them with a slotted spoon. Remove from the pan, drain on paper towels, and keep warm in a moderate oven while you cook the remaining pakoras. Allow the oil to come back to 350°F. between batches.

When all the vegetables are ready, garnish with lemon wedges and coriander or parsley and serve at once with the mango relish.

Mango Relish

Ingredients

RELISH	
¼ cup medium-sweet sherry	1 star anise
¼ cup water	½ teaspoon salt
¼ cup white wine vinegar	Pinch of ground mace
2 tablespoons sugar	1 mango, peeled, pitted, and diced
1 cinnamon stick	1 small red bell pepper, seeded and diced
	1 tablespoon lemon juice

Place the sherry, water, vinegar, sugar, cinnamon, star anise, salt, and mace in a small, heavy-bottomed saucepan. Bring to a boil and simmer over medium heat for 5 minutes. Add the mango, bell pepper, and lemon juice; lower the heat and simmer for 5 minutes more. Remove from the heat and let cool completely. Spoon into a screw top jar and refrigerate until required.

Alex's Zucchini with Pasta

SERVES 4

While I was working in Greece recently, Alex, the photographer's assistant, kept promising to cook his mother's recipe for zucchini with rosemary. On our last evening, he did, and it was well worth the wait. I serve this truly delicious combination with pasta.

Ingredients

4 to 5 cups dried pasta, such as
penne, rigatoni, or orecchiette
2 tablespoons lemon-scented
(or extra-virgin) olive oil
2 cloves garlic, finely chopped
4 medium zucchini, thinly sliced
1 tablespoon chopped fresh rosemary
Grated zest and juice of 2 lemons
½ cup pitted black olives
Salt and freshly ground black pepper

Bring a 3-quart saucepan of salted water to a boil, add the pasta, and return to a boil. Lower the heat and simmer uncovered for 10 to 12 minutes, or until the pasta is *al dente*—just done.

When the pasta is almost cooked, heat the olive oil in a large skillet and sauté the garlic over medium heat until it begins to brown. Add the zucchini, rosemary, and lemon zest and juice and stir-fry for 3 to 4 minutes, or until the zucchini are lightly browned and just tender. Stir in the olives, season to taste, and remove from the heat.

Drain the cooked pasta and toss with the zucchini until combined. Serve immediately.

Layered Vegetable Terrine

SERVES 8–10

The muted colors of this layered vegetable terrine echo the delicate flavors of the vegetables. Served with a simple carrot and chive salad, this makes a perfect light supper dish.

Preheat the oven to 375°F. Lightly oil and line the bottom of a 2-pound loaf pan with wax paper or parchment.

Steam the peas, chopped carrots, and cauliflower separately for 10 to 15 minutes, or until each is cooked. Let cool.

Puree the peas with 1 egg yolk, 2 tablespoons cream cheese, and 1 teaspoon lemon juice. Repeat with the carrots and then the cauliflower. Stir the chives into the pea puree, the almonds into the carrot puree, and the nutmeg into the cauliflower puree.

Whisk the egg whites until stiff, then carefully fold one-third into each puree until just combined. Season well and spoon the pea mousse into the prepared pan, carefully smoothing the surface. Top with the carrot mousse and then the cauliflower mousse, smoothing the surface of each. Cover with a piece of lightly oiled wax paper.

Place the loaf pan in a roasting pan and pour in boiling water to come two thirds of the way up the sides of the pan. Transfer to the oven and bake for 40 minutes. Remove the wax paper and cook for 10 to 15 minutes more, until the top feels firm to the touch. Remove from the oven and let cool in the pan on a wire rack.

Using a potato peeler, peel the whole carrots into thin strips and toss with the chives. Blend the oil, vinegar, and salt and pepper and mix with the carrot strips and chives.

Turn the terrine out of the pan and cut into slices. Serve with the salad.

Ingredients

TERRINE
2 cups (12 ounces) shelled peas
2 cups (12 ounces) chopped carrots
4 cups (12 ounces) cauliflower florets
3 eggs, separated
6 tablespoons low-fat cream cheese
3 teaspoons lemon juice
1 tablespoon chopped fresh chives
2 tablespoons ground almonds
¼ teaspoon freshly grated nutmeg
Salt and freshly ground white pepper

SALAD
3 large carrots, peeled
Small handful of fresh chives, snipped
2 tablespoons hazelnut oil
1 teaspoon raspberry vinegar
Salt and freshly ground black pepper

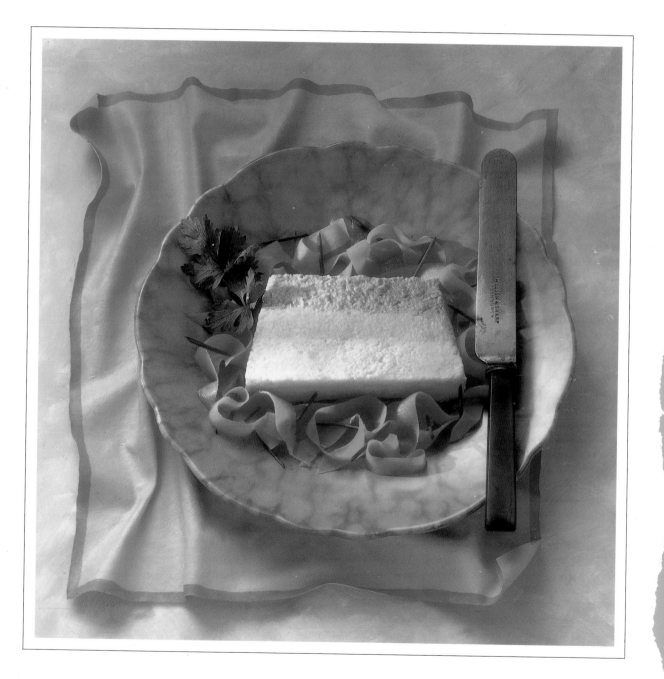

Mediterranean Tian

SERVES 4 – 6

A tian *is a Provençal earthenware casserole in which this layered ratatouille is baked. I was given a tian by a friend as a wedding present and I use it regularly. In this tasty vegetable dish the slices of tomato and zucchini are sprinkled with ground almonds as well as Parmesan cheese, which creates an unusual topping.*

Ingredients

1 small eggplant, diced
1 teaspoon salt
3 tablespoons olive oil
2 cloves garlic
1 red onion, thinly sliced
1 red bell pepper, seeded and thinly sliced
1 teaspoon fennel seeds
1 teaspoon chopped fresh rosemary
1 teaspoon chopped fresh thyme
¼ cup dry red wine

4 ripe medium tomatoes, coarsely chopped, plus 2 tomatoes, thinly sliced
2 tablespoons tomato paste
Pinch of sugar
Salt and freshly ground black pepper
1 large zucchini, thinly sliced
¼ cup freshly grated Parmesan cheese
¼ cup ground almonds
Salt and freshly ground pepper

Extra rosemary and thyme, to sprinkle

Preheat the oven to 350°F. Lightly oil a tian or shallow ovenproof dish.

Put the diced eggplant in a colander, sprinkle with salt, and let drain for 30 minutes.

Heat 1 tablespoon of the olive oil in a large skillet and sauté the garlic, onion, red pepper, fennel seeds, rosemary, and thyme for 5 minutes.

Wash the eggplant to remove the salt and dry thoroughly. Add to the pan with the wine, chopped tomatoes, tomato paste, sugar, and salt and pepper. Simmer over medium heat for 10 minutes, or until the mixture is thick and most of the liquid has evaporated.

Transfer the vegetables to the prepared dish. Arrange alternating circles of zucchini and tomato slices over the top and drizzle the zucchini with a little oil. Bake for 30 minutes.

Mix the cheese and almonds, then sprinkle on top along with salt and pepper and extra rosemary and thyme. Drizzle on the remaining oil and bake for a further 15 minutes, until bubbling and lightly golden.

Brown the top under a hot broiler, if desired. Serve the tian piping hot, warm, or cold.

Moroccan Vegetable Stew with Roasted Buckwheat

SERVES 6

I was first introduced to roasted buckwheat (kasha) while working on a Russian cookbook. Here it is served as an accompaniment to a Moroccan-style stew, which is more commonly served with couscous. The buckwheat, with its nutty texture and smoky flavor, combines with the spiced vegetables to create a wholesome and nourishing dish.

Ingredients

STEW

2 tablespoons olive oil
2 cloves garlic, coarsely chopped
1 teaspoon grated fresh ginger
1 teaspoon ground cumin
1 teaspoon ground cinnamon
½ teaspoon ground turmeric
2 small onions, quartered
3 medium carrots, coarsely chopped
4 baby turnips, trimmed and quartered
½ pound sweet potatoes, peeled and cubed
1 cup tomato juice
1 cup water
1½ cups cooked chick-peas

½ cup seedless raisins
2 small zucchini, thinly sliced
1½ cups button mushrooms,
  halved if large
2 tablespoons chopped fresh parsley
Salt and freshly ground black pepper

GRAIN

3 cups water
2½ cups roasted buckwheat (kasha)
2 tablespoons olive oil
½ teaspoon salt

½ cup cashew nuts, toasted
Parsley sprigs, for garnish

Heat the oil in a large skillet and sauté the garlic, ginger, cumin, cinnamon, and turmeric for 2 minutes. Add the onions, carrots, turnips, and potatoes and stir-fry for 5 minutes, or until all the vegetables are well coated with the spice mixture.

Add the tomato juice and water; bring to a boil, cover, and simmer gently for 15 minutes. Add the chick-peas, raisins, zucchini, mushrooms, and parsley and simmer for 15 minutes more. Season to taste.

Meanwhile, prepare the buckwheat. Bring the water to a boil in a heavy-bottomed 2-quart saucepan. Add the buckwheat and oil, cover, and simmer over very low heat for 15 minutes. Do not remove the lid during this time.

Stir the salt into the buckwheat and pile it onto a large serving dish. Spoon the vegetables over it. Sprinkle with the cashew nuts, and serve the vegetable juices separately. Garnish with the parsley sprigs.

Radicchio, Artichoke, and Goat Cheese Pizza

SERVES 4

I cannot remember when I ate my first pizza, but I distinctly remember eating a variation of this one. While staying with friends in France, I was served this delicious pizza with its topping of bitter radicchio, creamy goat cheese, and nutty artichokes. It is a definite must for pizza lovers everywhere.

Ingredients

DOUGH
1¼ teaspoons active dry yeast
1¼ cups tepid water
3 cups all-purpose flour
Pinch of sugar
½ teaspoon salt

TOMATO SAUCE
2 tablespoons olive oil
2 cloves garlic, crushed
8 medium tomatoes,
peeled, seeded, and chopped
1 tablespoon chopped fresh oregano

TOPPING
12 young artichokes,
about 3 inches long
Juice of ½ lemon

Oil for brushing
1 small radicchio,
separated into leaves
6 ounces goat cheese, crumbled
Greek olives

Blend the yeast with the water, ½ cup flour, and the sugar and leave in a warm place for 10 minutes, or until frothy. Sift the remaining flour and salt into a bowl. Make a well in the center and work in the yeast mixture. Knead for 8 to 10 minutes, or until the dough is smooth and elastic. Place in an oiled bowl, turning to coat well, cover, and let rise in a warm place for 30 minutes, until doubled in size.

Meanwhile, make the tomato sauce. Heat the oil in a small saucepan and sauté the garlic for 2 minutes. Stir in the remaining ingredients and simmer gently, uncovered, for 15 minutes, until thick. Let cool.

Preheat the oven to 475°F. Lightly oil four 8-inch pizza pans or 2 large baking sheets.

continued

Cut off all but ¼ inch of stalk from the artichokes and discard. Using a small knife, snip off the tough outer leaves until only the tender inner leaves remain. Trim the top two-thirds of the artichokes and discard. Cut in half, rub all over with lemon juice, and blanch in boiling water for 3 to 4 minutes, until just tender. Refresh under cold water and pat dry.

Punch the dough down on a lightly floured surface and divide into 4 equal pieces. Roll out to 8-inch rounds and place in the pizza pans or on the baking sheets. Brush crusts with a little oil and spread on the tomato sauce. Top each pizza with 3 to 4 radicchio leaves and 6 artichoke halves. Sprinkle the cheese and plenty of olives over the top.

Bake the pizzas in the top of the oven for 10 to 15 minutes, until bubbling and golden. Serve at once with a mixed salad.

Note: If fresh young artichokes are not available, use good-quality canned or frozen artichoke hearts instead.

Stuffed Mediterranean Vegetables

SERVES 6

Hollowed-out vegetables make ideal containers for any number of different fillings. Goat cheese and sun-dried tomatoes are a particular favorite of mine, and make a regular supper dish.

Ingredients

VEGETABLES	
½ cup bulgur	2 medium red onions, unpeeled
1 small eggplant	2 large, ripe tomatoes
½ teaspoon salt	1 orange or red bell pepper

Soak the bulgur in cold water for 10 minutes. Drain and set aside.

Cut the eggplant in half lengthwise, sprinkle with salt, and leave in a colander to drain for 30 minutes.

Preheat the oven to 400°F.

Put the onions in a 2-quart saucepan and cover with cold water. Bring to a boil, lower the heat, and simmer, uncovered, for 15 minutes. Drain and refresh under cold water until cool enough to handle. Cut the onions in half vertically through the stem and root ends. Scoop out most of the flesh, leaving the skin and 1 or 2 layers of flesh intact. Chop the scooped-out flesh and reserve.

Slice the tomatoes in half vertically through the stalk and gently squeeze out the seeds and juice. Discard. Carefully scrape out all the pulp, leaving the shell intact. Chop and reserve the pulp.

Slice the pepper in half vertically, scoop out the seeds, and discard.

Wash the salted eggplant, pat dry, and scoop out the flesh, leaving a thin layer over the skins. Chop the flesh and reserve.

Stuffing

Ingredients

STUFFING
2 tablespoons olive oil
2 cloves garlic, crushed
1 tablespoon chopped fresh sage
1 tablespoon chopped fresh basil
¼ cup sun-dried tomatoes packed in oil, drained and finely chopped
2 cups chopped mushrooms

¼ cup pine nuts, toasted (*page 8*)
2 cups (8 ounces) diced mozzarella cheese
Salt and freshly ground black pepper
¼ cup freshly grated Parmesan cheese or fresh whole wheat bread crumbs

Heat 1 tablespoon of the oil in a large skillet and sauté the garlic, chopped onion flesh, sage, basil, and sun-dried tomatoes for 5 minutes. Remove from the pan with a slotted spoon and place in a large bowl. Heat the remaining oil in the skillet and stir-fry the mushrooms and chopped eggplant for 5 minutes. Stir into the onion mixture and cool slightly. Stir in the drained bulgur, pine nuts, mozzarella, and plenty of salt and pepper.

Spoon the stuffing into the vegetable shells, sprinkle with cheese or bread crumbs, and bake the stuffed eggplant, onion, and pepper shells for 20 minutes. Add the tomato pulp, drizzle with a little oil, and bake for 15 minutes more, until the vegetables are tender. (Test with the point of a sharp knife.)

Serve the vegetables hot, with a crisp green salad.

Warm Mushroom Salad

SERVES 4

The natural flavor of wild mushrooms is so wonderful that I prefer to serve them simply sautéed with butter or oil, a little garlic, and fresh herbs, providing a quite delicious medley of earthy flavors. Try serving them with Griddled Polenta with Herbs (page 85) or Potato and Scallion Latkes (page 77).

Ingredients

4 tablespoons (½ stick) butter or extra-virgin olive oil
1¾ to 2 pounds mixed wild mushrooms (cèpes, chanterelles, morels, oyster, shiitake)
2 cloves garlic, finely chopped

1 tablespoon chopped fresh thyme
Squeeze of lemon juice
Salt and freshly ground black pepper
1 tablespoon chopped fresh parsley

Heat the butter or oil in a large nonstick skillet, and sauté the mushrooms, garlic, and thyme over medium heat for 3 to 4 minutes, or until the mushrooms are just soft and begin to release their juices.

Transfer to a serving plate, pour over the pan juices, and squeeze the lemon juice over all. Season to taste and sprinkle with parsley before serving.

Vegetable Accompaniments

Sweet Potatoes en Papillote

It is always fun to be served a golden parcel straight from the oven, and I find baking sweet potatoes this way to be very successful.

Ingredients

8 tablespoons (1 stick) butter, softened

2 pounds sweet potatoes, peeled and cubed

18 cloves garlic, unpeeled

6 sprigs fresh tarragon

Salt and freshly ground black pepper

Preheat the oven to 400°F.

Cut 6 large heart-shaped pieces of wax paper, approximately 10 inches long and 12 inches wide. Make a fold line down the center, open out flat, and spread both sides with a little softened butter. Divide the remaining ingredients equally among the hearts, placing the ingredients on one side of the fold, and dot with the remaining butter. Fold the other side over and turn under both edges together all the way around to enclose the filling completely.

Place on a baking sheet and bake for 20 to 25 minutes. Check one parcel to ensure the potatoes are cooked, then serve the parcels straight from the oven.

Note: For a dish with less cholesterol, substitute extra-virgin olive oil for the butter. Brush each parcel with a little oil and drizzle the filling liberally, then bake as above.

Potato and Scallion Latkes

SERVES 4–6

Savory potato pancakes with the addition of shredded scallions provide a tasty accompaniment to many dishes. They are also delicious served with a spoonful of crème fraîche and apple sauce.

Ingredients

1½ pounds baking potatoes (Russets)
1 cup finely shredded scallions
2 teaspoons mustard seeds
1 teaspoon salt
2 eggs, lightly beaten
2 tablespoons all-purpose flour

2 to 3 tablespoons hazelnut or peanut oil for frying

Peel and coarsely grate the potatoes, squeeze out as much liquid as possible, and place in a large bowl. Stir in the scallions, mustard seeds, and salt. Using a fork or your hands, stir in the eggs and flour until evenly distributed.

Heat 1 tablespoon of the oil in a nonstick skillet or griddle over medium heat. Drop on 3 separate tablespoons of potato mixture and flatten each with a spatula to form small pancakes about 4 inches across.

Fry for 2 to 3 minutes, until golden. Flip the pancakes and fry for 2 to 3 minutes on the other side. Drain on paper towels and keep warm. Repeat to make 12 pancakes.

Serve hot with a spoonful of crème fraîche, apple sauce, or as a side dish to the Warm Mushroom Salad (*page 72*).

Fava Beans with Lemon-Butter Sauce

SERVES 4

I prefer to peel the tough outer skins of fava beans. Although this is time-consuming, you will find it is worth the effort when you try this dish. Be patient—you will be well rewarded. The sauce is rich and creamy, so this dish is best served with a crisp green salad or as an accompaniment to a selection of vegetables.

Ingredients

4 pounds fava beans, shelled
8 tablespoons (1 stick) unsalted butter
1 large leek, trimmed and thinly sliced
1 clove garlic, crushed
2 tablespoons chopped fresh mint
2 tablespoons lemon juice
4 tablespoon half-and-half
Salt and freshly ground black pepper

Blanch the shelled beans in boiling water for 1 minute. Refresh under cold water, drain, and pat dry. Remove the hard outer skins from the beans and discard.

Melt half the butter in a skillet and sauté the leek and garlic for 3 to 4 minutes, or until soft. Stir in the mint and peeled beans, cover, and simmer over very low heat for 5 minutes.

Strain the juices into a small pan and keep the beans warm. Simmer the juices and stir in the lemon juice. Gradually whisk in the remaining butter and half-and-half until the sauce becomes thick and glossy. Season to taste with salt and pepper, stir in the fava beans, and heat through.

Serve immediately with a salad.

Chilled Marinated Vegetables

SERVES 4

These chilled vegetables in a lightly spiced saffron stock make a delightful summer supper dish. Be careful not to overcook the vegetables, because their crisp texture is vital to the success of this recipe.

Ingredients

¼ cup extra-virgin olive oil
6 pearl onions, halved
2 young leeks, trimmed and cut into 1-inch slices
4 cloves garlic, whole
2 cups cauliflower florets (6 ounces)
2 celery stalks, thickly sliced
4 ounces button mushrooms, wiped clean
Small handful of snap beans
1 tablespoon dill seed
¾ cup dry white wine

½ cup water
Juice of ½ lemon
Pinch of saffron strands
2 bay leaves
½ teaspoon salt
1 tablespoon white wine vinegar
1 tablespoon chopped celery leaves
1 tablespoon chopped fresh parsley
2 teaspoons chopped fresh dill
1 tablespoon capers
6 white peppercorns

Heat the oil in a large skillet, add the vegetables and dill seed, and sauté over medium heat for 3 to 4 minutes, or until well coated with oil.

Add the wine, water, lemon juice, saffron, bay leaves, and salt; bring to a boil, cover, and simmer over low heat for 8 to 10 minutes, or until the vegetables are just cooked. Remove the vegetables with a slotted spoon and place in a shallow dish. Let cool completely.

Increase the heat and reduce the cooking liquid for 5 minutes, or until you are left with about 1 cup. Remove from the heat, cool slightly, and add the remaining ingredients. Pour over the vegetables and set aside until completely cold.

Marinate overnight in the refrigerator. Serve slightly chilled.

Fennel Gratin

This rich and creamy baked fennel, with the slightest hint of garlic, makes a memorable side dish for any occasion.

Ingredients

1 clove garlic	1½ cups heavy cream
2 pounds fennel (4 large bulbs)	Pinch of ground mace
2 teaspoons chopped fresh thyme	Salt and freshly ground white pepper
½ cup crumbled goat cheese	

Preheat the oven to 400°F.

Cut the garlic clove in half and rub all over the inside of a gratin dish.

Quarter and slice the fennel thinly. In a small bowl, combine the fennel and thyme, and carefully stir in the cheese, cream, and seasonings. Do not overmix. Spoon into the prepared gratin dish and bake for 30 to 35 minutes, until bubbling and golden. Test the fennel with a pointed knife to make sure it is tender.

Serve piping hot.

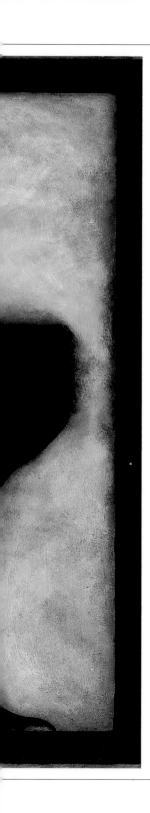

Grilled Eggplants with Pistachio and Mint Salsa

SERVES 6

If you have ever been fortunate enough to sit down to a table of Italian antipasto dishes,
you have probably experienced the pleasures of grilled eggplants. The flesh absorbs the
smoky charbroiled flavor and becomes soft and creamy. I experimented with several
different salsas before combining pistachios and fresh mint to
make this mouth-watering and unusual sauce.

Ingredients

12 small eggplants
(3 to 4 inches in length)
Salt

SALSA
¼ cup shelled pistachio nuts
½ cup loosely packed mint leaves
¼ cup loosely packed parsley leaves

1 clove garlic, coarsely chopped
2 scallions, trimmed and coarsely chopped
¾ cup extra-virgin olive oil
2 tablespoons white wine vinegar
¼ teaspoon sugar
Salt and freshly ground black pepper

Cut the eggplants in half lengthwise, sprinkle liberally with salt, and let drain in a colander for 30 minutes.

Blanch the pistachio nuts in boiling water for 30 seconds. Refresh under cold water, drain well, and pat dry. Rub the nuts in a clean dish towel to remove their skins.

Blend the nuts, mint, parsley, garlic, and scallions to form a fairly smooth paste. Stir in the remaining ingredients and let infuse.

Preheat the broiler.

Wash the eggplants thoroughly and dry well. Brush with oil and place under the broiler, cut side down, for 4 to 5 minutes, or until the skins blister and become charred. Turn over, brush with a little more oil, and broil for 1 minute, or until the flesh browns.

Serve hot with plenty of salsa.

Spinach Balls in Olive Oil

SERVES 4–6

These cold balls of spinach absorb the flavors of the olive oil, lemon, and spices, making them refreshingly fragrant. Serve them with a spoonful of crème fraîche or yogurt.

Ingredients

SPINACH
1½ pounds spinach leaves, washed
1 tablespoon olive oil
1 teaspoon salt

MARINADE
½ cup extra-virgin olive oil
Juice of 1 lemon
1 clove garlic, crushed
1 teaspoon ground coriander
½ teaspoon ground cumin
Pinch of freshly grated nutmeg
Salt and freshly ground black pepper

Bring a large saucepan of water to a boil. Add the spinach, oil, and salt and simmer, covered, for 10 minutes, or until the spinach is very soft. Drain and refresh under cold water, until the spinach is cool enough to handle.

Squeeze out all the liquid and form the spinach into 12 small balls the size of large walnuts, and place in a shallow dish.

Blend the olive oil, lemon juice, garlic, coriander, cumin, and nutmeg together. Season with salt and pepper and pour over the spinach. Cover and set aside to marinate for several hours or overnight in a cool place, but not in the refrigerator. Turn the balls over from time to time.

Serve the spinach balls with a selection of other salads or vegetable dishes and crusty bread.

Griddled Polenta with Herbs

SERVES 8–12

Polenta, made from cornmeal, is served plain as a staple accompaniment to many Italian stews and meat dishes, or—as in this recipe—it is allowed to set, cut into rounds, and seared on a griddle. The addition of herbs, garlic, and Parmesan cheese makes these small, golden cakes irresistible.

Ingredients

1 quart water
2 teaspoons salt
1 cup polenta (coarse yellow cornmeal)
2 tablespoons chopped fresh herbs
2 tablespoons (¼ stick) butter
½ cup freshly grated Parmesan cheese

Lightly oil a shallow 9-inch square tin.

Bring the water and salt to a boil in a 3-quart saucepan, slowly whisk in the polenta and herbs, lower the heat, and simmer gently, uncovered, for 30 minutes. Stir frequently. Remove from the heat and stir in the butter and cheese.

Spoon the polenta into the prepared tin, smooth the surface, and let cool completely.

Turn the polenta out onto a chopping board and, using a round cookie cutter, cut out 2½-inch rounds.

Heat a griddle over medium heat and brush with a little oil. Fry the polenta rounds for 2 to 3 minutes on each side, until golden.

Serve hot.

Baked Beets

SERVES 4 – 8

I think that beets are the most underrated of all vegetables. Perhaps this is due to the jars of sliced beets, saturated with vinegar, which are so commonly sold in our shops. Try this method of baking them whole in their skins and discover a whole new vegetable.

Ingredients

8 medium raw beets
(4 ounces each)

DRESSING
1 cup *fromage blanc* or
plain yogurt
4 tablespoons chopped
fresh chives
Salt and freshly ground black pepper

Preheat the oven to 350°F.

Wash the beets carefully to remove any trapped earth, without tearing their skins. Dry well and place in a roasting pan. Loosely cover with aluminum foil and bake for 1½ to 2 hours, until the skins break easily if pressed lightly with a finger and come easily away from the flesh.

Meanwhile, prepare the dressing. Mix together the *fromage blanc* and chives and season to taste. Cover and let infuse.

Remove the beets from the oven, peel, and slice in half. Place on serving plates, spoon the dressing over the beets, and serve hot.

Baked Baby Vegetables with Citrus

SERVES 6

The vegetables are baked in small foil parcels, which seal in their flavor. The tangy citrus sauce glazes them as they cook, making an exquisite and unusual dish.

Ingredients

4 tablespoons (½ stick)
unsalted butter
6 cloves garlic, unpeeled
8 pearl onions, halved
4 baby fennel bulbs, quartered
18 baby carrots, trimmed
18 baby parsnips
8 baby turnips, trimmed and halved
6 sprigs thyme
12 kumquats, halved
2 tablespoons brandy
½ cup orange juice
½ cup vegetable stock or water
1 tablespoon honey
1 cup cooked chestnuts
Salt and freshly ground pepper

Cut aluminum foil into six 12-inch squares.

Preheat the oven to 400°F. and turn the edges of the foil up to form bowl-shaped containers.

Heat half the butter in a large skillet and sauté the garlic, onions, fennel, and carrots over medium heat for 5 minutes, or until lightly browned.

Add the parsnips, turnips, and thyme and sauté for 2 to 3 minutes more. With a slotted spoon, transfer the vegetables to the prepared foil containers.

Add the remaining butter and the kumquats to the skillet and sauté for 2 to 3 minutes, or until lightly browned. Add to the vegetables.

Pour the brandy, orange juice, stock, and honey into the pan; bring to a boil, and cook over high heat for 3 to 4 minutes, or until reduced to about 6 tablespoons. Spoon a tablespoon into each foil container and add the chestnuts and seasonings.

Pull the edges of the foil together and turn them over to seal in the vegetables and their juices completely. Place in a large baking pan and bake for 20 minutes. Remove the parcels from the oven, and serve straight from the foil or transfer to serving plates.

Serve hot. These vegetables are very good served with a crusty bread and a crisp salad.

See photograph on page 134

Braised Red Cabbage in Wine and Port

SERVES 6 – 8

The red cabbage develops a deep, rich flavor as it is braised slowly in red wine and port.

Ingredients

1 tablespoon olive oil	¾ cup red wine
1 large onion, thinly sliced	¼ cup ruby port wine
1½ pounds red cabbage, finely shredded	2 tablespoons red wine vinegar
1 tablespoon chopped fresh thyme	1 cup walnut halves
1 teaspoon caraway seeds	½ cup golden raisins
10 juniper berries, crushed	Salt and freshly ground black pepper

Heat the oil in a large skillet and sauté the onion for 5 minutes, until soft. Stir in the cabbage, thyme, caraway seeds, and juniper berries and sauté for 5 minutes more.

Add the wines and vinegar; cover and simmer gently for 20 minutes.

Add the walnuts and raisins, cover, and simmer for 10 to 15 minutes more, until the cabbage is tender. Adjust the seasonings and serve hot.

VEGETABLE ACCOMPANIMENTS
89

Stir-fried Sesame Cabbage with Ginger

SERVES 4

The Chinese treat their vegetables with a great deal of respect, stir-frying them quickly over high heat. In this recipe, the vegetables absorb the rich flavor of the spicy sauce while retaining their own flavor and crisp texture. It's a delicious combination.

Ingredients

2 teaspoons roasted sesame oil
2 teaspoons peanut oil
1 ½-inch piece fresh ginger, peeled and cut into thin strips
1 large clove garlic, sliced
2 medium zucchini, thinly sliced
1 small green cabbage, thinly shredded
1 tablespoon chopped fresh coriander (cilantro)
Grated zest and juice of 1 lime
1 cup unsalted peanuts, toasted
2 tablespoons sesame seeds, toasted
Salt and freshly ground Szechuan pepper

Heat the oils in a wok or large skillet over high heat and stir-fry the ginger and garlic for 1 minute. Add the zucchini, cabbage, and coriander and stir-fry for 3 to 4 minutes, or until the cabbage just begins to wilt.

Remove from the heat, transfer to a large bowl, and stir in the lime juice and zest, peanuts, and sesame seeds. Season with salt and pepper and serve immediately.

Salads

Tubbs's Tomato Salad

This is simply the most wonderful salad I have ever tasted, and the credit must go to my great friend Tubbs. He served this tomato salad as a side dish at a barbecue last summer and it was the star of the show. He was glad to pass on the recipe, which is great news to all who are inspired to make it.

Ingredients

8 large, ripe tomatoes, thinly sliced
8 yellow cherry tomatoes, thinly sliced
8 sun-dried tomatoes in oil, drained and thinly sliced
Grated zest of 2 lemons

Small handful of basil leaves, shredded
3 tablespoons extra-virgin olive oil
1 tablespoon balsamic vinegar
Salt and freshly ground black pepper

Arrange the tomato slices in rings on a serving plate. Scatter with the lemon zest and basil leaves, and drizzle with the oil and vinegar.

Season generously with salt and pepper, cover, and let marinate for 30 minutes before serving.

Simple Summer Salad

Use a selection of your favorite salad greens and herbs in this simplest of salads.
The flowers add color as well as a subtle flavor.

Ingredients

SALAD	DRESSING
4 large handfuls of mixed salad greens (bibb, romaine, chicory, lamb's lettuce, escarole, red oak leaf, *lollo rosso*)	4 tablespoons extra-virgin olive oil
	1 teaspoon balsamic vinegar
	½ clove garlic, crushed
8 tablespoons chopped fresh herbs (basil, chervil, chives, lemon balm, lovage, mint, summer savory)	1 teaspoon Dijon mustard
	Pinch of sugar
Handful of mixed edible flowers (nasturtiums, borage, pansies, rose petals, violas)	Salt and freshly ground black pepper

Just before serving, toss the greens, herbs, and
flowers together in a large bowl. Blend the
dressing together, pour over the salad, mix well
to coat, and serve immediately.

Beet and Grapefruit Salad

SERVES 4

Beets were the very first vegetable I managed to grow when I was small. I was given a section of my parents garden to "mess around in," and much to everyone's surprise— not least my own—I succeeded in growing two beets, of which I was extremely proud. I have had a passion for the vegetable ever since.

Ingredients

SALAD	DRESSING
3 cups cooked beets, peeled and diced	3 tablespoons *fromage blanc* or yogurt cheese *(page 8)*
Large handful of lamb's lettuce (mâche)	3 tablespoons walnut oil
Large bunch of watercress	2 teaspoons cider vinegar
1 small red onion, thinly sliced	2 teaspoons grated horseradish
2 ruby grapefruit, peeled and segmented	2 teaspoons chopped fresh tarragon
½ cup chopped walnuts, toasted	Salt and freshly ground black pepper

Place the beets, lamb's lettuce, watercress, onion, and grapefruit in a large bowl.

Blend the dressing ingredients together, season to taste, and pour over the salad. Toss well until mixed.

Serve the salad at once, sprinkled with the walnuts.

Mango and Hazelnut Salad

SERVES 4 – 6

This colorful summer salad contains a kaleidoscope of greens and oranges. The leaves and vegetables are tossed with my favorite salad dressing: hazelnut oil and raspberry vinegar, sweetened with a little honey. Vary the amount of honey to suit your taste, and use an assortment of salad greens such as oak leaf, bibb, romaine, watercress, arugula, and spinach.

Ingredients

SALAD
½ cup snow peas, trimmed
½ cup snap beans or baby green beans, trimmed
Assortment of salad greens (large handful per person)
1 large mango, peeled, pit removed, and flesh sliced
1 orange bell pepper, seeded and sliced

¼ cup hazelnuts, toasted and coarsely chopped

DRESSING
3 tablespoons hazelnut oil
2 teaspoons raspberry vinegar
½ to 1 teaspoon honey
Salt and freshly ground black pepper

Blanch the snow peas and beans in boiling water for 1 to 2 minutes, until just tender. Drain, refresh under cold water, drain again, and pat dry. Place in a large bowl and add the greens, mango, and pepper. Reserve the hazelnuts.

Blend the oil, vinegar, honey, and salt and pepper together and pour over the salad. Toss well to coat the leaves and serve at once, sprinkled with the chopped hazelnuts.

Lentil and Sweet Pepper Salad

SERVES 4–6

For this hearty salad, the cooked lentils are tossed with the dressing while still hot, so they absorb as much flavor as possible.

Ingredients

3 bell peppers, 1 each red, yellow, and orange
1¼ cups green lentils, washed
3 cups water
1 small onion, peeled
1 clove garlic, peeled

DRESSING
¼ cup extra-virgin olive oil
Juice of 1 lemon
2 cloves garlic, crushed

1 tablespoon chopped fresh coriander (cilantro)
1 tablespoon chopped fresh parsley
2 teaspoons ground cumin
Salt and freshly ground pepper

1 small red chili pepper, seeded and finely chopped
1 small red onion, thinly sliced
½ cup dried apricots, thinly sliced
Salt and freshly ground black pepper

Heat the broiler.

Broil the peppers until charred and blistered on all sides. Tie in a plastic bag or place in a covered dish and let cool to loosen skins.

Put the lentils, water, onion, and garlic into a 2-quart saucepan. Bring to a boil, lower the heat, and simmer, uncovered, for 20 to 25 minutes, or until the lentils are tender but still a little crunchy. Drain and place in a large bowl.

Meanwhile, make the dressing. Blend the oil, lemon juice, garlic, coriander, parsley, and cumin, and season with salt and pepper. Drain the lentils, discard the onion and garlic, and place the lentils in a large bowl. Stir in the dressing and set aside.

Peel and seed the bell peppers over a bowl to catch any juices, slice the flesh thinly, and reserve. Pour any juices into the lentils and leave to cool completely.

Stir the bell peppers, chili peppers, onion, apricot slices, and salt and pepper to taste into the lentils and serve at once.

Mixed Baby Vegetable Salad with Tomato-Herb Dressing

SERVES 6

A selection of lightly blanched vegetables, tossed in a piquant tomato and herb dressing, makes a refreshing side salad or a light luncheon dish. Use seasonal herbs and vegetables of your choice—these are only a suggestion.

Ingredients

DRESSING	SALAD
2 large tomatoes, peeled, seeded, and diced	4 ounces fresh oyster or shiitake mushrooms
2 tablespoons chopped fresh herbs (basil, chives, tarragon, chervil)	6 baby artichokes, trimmed *(page 68)* and sprinkled with juice of ½ lemon
9 tablespoons light olive oil	1½ pounds mixed vegetables (corn kernels, carrots, snow peas, snap beans, asparagus tips)
2 tablespoons white wine vinegar	
Pinch of sugar	
Pinch of cayenne pepper	
Salt	

Blend the tomatoes, herbs, oil, vinegar, sugar, cayenne, and salt together in a small bowl. Place the mushrooms in a shallow dish and spoon 3 to 4 tablespoons of dressing over them. Let marinate while preparing the remaining vegetables.

Trim and halve the remaining vegetables as necessary. Bring a 3-quart saucepan of water to a boil and blanch the vegetables in separate batches, for 1 to 2 minutes, or until tender—the artichokes may need to be cooked a little longer. Rinse under cold water to prevent further cooking, drain well, and dry on paper towels.

Place the vegetables in a large bowl, add the marinated mushrooms, and pour the remaining dressing over them. Toss well until the vegetables are coated and serve immediately.

Ma's Monday Salad

Every Monday, my parents finished off the traditional Sunday roast with a home-grown salad for lunch. This is typical of the salads my mother would serve, with a few additions of my own.

Ingredients

SALAD	DRESSING
8 small new potatoes, scrubbed	¼ cup extra-virgin olive oil
1 cup snow peas, trimmed	2 tablespoons crème fraîche
¾ cup corn kernels (1 medium ear)	or yogurt cheese (*page 8*)
6 large ripe tomatoes, quartered	1 tablespoon whole-grain mustard
1 cup cooked butter beans or lima beans	2 teaspoons chopped fresh chives
½ cup pitted black olives	2 teaspoons white wine vinegar
2 slices thick white bread,	Salt and freshly ground black pepper
toasted and crumbled	
	3 hard-cooked eggs, shelled and quartered

Cook the potatoes in boiling salted water for 10 to 12 minutes, or until tender. Drain, refresh under cold water to prevent them from cooking further, and pat dry.

Blanch the snow peas and corn in plenty of salted boiling water for 2 minutes, until just tender. Drain, refresh under cold water, and dry.

Mix the potatoes, snow peas, and corn with the tomatoes, beans, olives, and bread.

Blend the dressing ingredients together, pour over the salad, and top with the egg quarters.

Serve at once.

Oriental-Style Broccoli Salad

SERVES 4

The spicy Chinese flavors of the dressing permeate the broccoli as it cools. The remaining salad ingredients add a crisp coolness to the dish, making it exceptionally tasty.

Ingredients

1 pound broccoli florets

DRESSING
1 tablespoon peanut oil
1 tablespoon roasted sesame oil
1 tablespoon balsamic vinegar
1 tablespoon soy sauce
2 teaspoons honey
½ teaspoon grated fresh ginger

1 clove garlic, crushed
Pinch of five-spice powder
Freshly ground Szechuan pepper

SALAD
1 large carrot
1 3-inch piece daikon (Asian white radish)
4 scallions, thickly sliced
½ cup dried coconut, toasted

Steam the broccoli for 5 to 7 minutes, or until just tender; be careful not to overcook it, since it will become mushy. Place in a large bowl.

Blend the peanut oil, sesame oil, vinegar, soy sauce, honey, ginger, garlic, five-spice powder, and Szechuan pepper and pour over the broccoli, mixing carefully until the broccoli is well coated. Let cool completely.

Cut the carrot in half and, using a potato peeler, peel the carrot into thin slivers. Prepare the daikon in the same way and add both to the cold broccoli with the scallions. Scatter the toasted coconut over the salad and serve at once.

Gem Salad

SERVES 4–6

This fresh summer salad, containing several different kinds of greens, is served with a tangy lime dressing. Gem lettuce is a long-leaf lettuce, much like a baby romaine or the heart of a regular romaine, which can be substituted if you can't find gem lettuce.

Ingredients

SALAD	DRESSING
4 ounces snap beans, trimmed and halved	6 tablespoons extra-virgin olive oil
4 gem lettuces, quartered	2 tablespoons plain yogurt
2 young leeks, trimmed and thinly sliced	2 tablespoons lime juice
4 scallions, trimmed and thinly sliced	1 teaspoon honey
2 ripe pears, peeled, cored, and sliced	Salt and freshly ground black pepper
1 tablespooon sunflower seeds, toasted	
1 tablespoon chopped fresh mint	

Blanch the beans in plenty of boiling, salted water for 2 minutes, or until just tender but still crunchy. Drain, refresh under cold water, and pat dry.

Place the beans in a large bowl; add the lettuce, leeks, scallions, pears, sunflower seeds, and mint and toss until well mixed.

Blend the olive oil, yogurt, lime juice, honey, and salt and pepper to taste until combined.

Arrange the salad on individual plates and drizzle a little dressing over each one. Serve immediately.

Radicchio and Melon Salad

SERVES 4

The bitter radicchio and sweet melon combine well in this attractive composed salad,
which was inspired by a dish often seen on Italian trattoria menus.

Ingredients

MAYONNAISE	SALAD
1 egg yolk	1 medium head radicchio
1 tablespoon lemon juice	A little olive oil and balsamic vinegar
½ teaspoon Dijon mustard	to drizzle
Pinch of sugar	1 small cantaloupe
Salt and freshly ground black pepper	1 large avocado
1 tablespoon chopped fresh chives	1 cup finely shredded fennel
1 cup light olive oil	

Make the mayonnaise. Place the egg yolk, lemon juice, mustard, sugar, and salt and pepper in a large bowl and beat together until pale and creamy. Stir in the chives. With a wire whisk, gradually beat in the oil a few drops at a time, in a steady stream, until the mixture is smooth and creamy. Do not add the oil too quickly or the mixture will break, and you will have to start again. Cover and set aside until the mayonnaise is required.

Tear the radicchio leaves into bite-size pieces, wash well, pat dry, and place in a bowl. Drizzle with a little olive oil and balsamic vinegar. Cut the cantaloupe in half, scoop out and discard the seeds, and cut the flesh into small pieces. Cut the avocado into quarters, discard the pit, and peel and slice the flesh lengthwise.

Arrange the radicchio, melon, avocado, and shredded fennel on serving plates, and spoon the mayonnaise over them.

Serve immediately.

Orange Pasta Salad

SERVES 6–8

*This tangy, orange-flavored pasta salad also features carrot sticks and caraway seeds.
The flavors combine perfectly to create a refreshingly different pasta salad.*

Ingredients

SALAD	DRESSING
4 cups dried pasta, such as penne or rigatoni	⅓ cup hazelnut oil
A little olive oil	¼ cup fresh orange juice
2 large carrots, cut into matchsticks	2 tablespoons raspberry vinegar
Grated zest of 1 orange	Salt and freshly ground black pepper
1 tablespoon caraway seeds	
1 tablespoon chopped fresh thyme	
1 cup slivered almonds	

Bring a large pot of water to a boil, add the pasta and a little olive oil, and return to a boil. Lower the heat and simmer gently, uncovered, for 10 to 12 minutes, or until the pasta is *al dente* (just done), then drain.

Meanwhile, put the carrots, orange zest, caraway seeds, and thyme into a large bowl. Set the almonds aside.

Blend the hazelnut oil, orange juice, and vinegar together, then season with salt and pepper. Pour over the salad mixture. Add the cooked pasta to the bowl. Toss until the pasta is well coated with the dressing. Set aside until cool.

Serve the salad sprinkled with the almonds.

An Astipálaian Salad

Astipálaia is a remote Greek island in the Aegean. I recently spent some time working there and was treated to a wonderfully fresh-tasting feta salad. Here is my version, to which I have added diced papaya.

Ingredients

DRESSING	SALAD
3 tablespoons extra-virgin olive oil	1½ cups crumbled feta cheese
2 tablespoons lemon juice	½ large cucumber, peeled and diced
1 clove garlic, crushed	1 tablespoon chopped fresh dill
Pinch of cayenne pepper	1 large papaya
Pinch of nutmeg	¼ cup pitted black Greek olives

Blend the dressing ingredients together and pour two-thirds of the dressing into a bowl. Add the feta, cucumber, and dill; stir well, cover, and set aside to marinate for several hours at room temperature.

To serve, peel the papaya, cut it in half, and scoop out and discard all of the seeds. Cut the flesh into bite-size pieces and mix with the remaining dressing.

Arrange the papaya and olives around the edge of a serving platter. Spoon the marinated feta mixture into the center and serve at once.

Breads

Focaccia

Sicily was the first place I visited on the continent, and I can still vividly recall the wonderful smell of baking bread each morning. It was also the first time I had eaten the Italian flat bread focaccia. Here, it is simply sprinkled with sea salt, but you can also find it covered with chopped sage or rosemary, or with chopped olives and garlic.

Focaccia is best eaten warm. It should be wrapped in a clean linen towel to cool; this makes it light and soft, but also means that it is best eaten the same day. However, if cut in half horizontally, focaccia makes delicious toast should there be any left over.

Blend the yeast with the water, ½ cup flour, and the sugar. Set aside in a warm place for 10 minutes, until frothy.

Sift the remaining flour and the salt into a large bowl. Make a well in the center and work in the frothed yeast mixture and olive oil to form a soft dough. Knead for 8 to 10 minutes, or until the dough is smooth and elastic. Place in an oiled bowl, turning to coat the dough, cover, and let rise in a warm place for 35 to 40 minutes, or until doubled in size.

Preheat the oven to 450°F. and lightly oil a large baking sheet.

Ingredients

1¼ teaspoons active dry yeast
1¼ cups tepid water
3 cups all-purpose flour
Pinch of sugar
1 teaspoon salt
¼ cup extra-virgin olive oil
Sea salt

Punch the dough down on a lightly floured surface and roll out to a rectangle about ½ inch thick. Transfer to the prepared baking sheet, brush with oil, and press small indentations all over the surface of the dough with your fingers. Cover and let rise for 30 minutes more.

Sprinkle the dough liberally with sea salt and bake for 20 to 25 minutes, until golden. Remove from the oven and wrap in a clean towel to cool.

Serve the bread while it is still warm as an accompaniment to soups, salads, or on its own.

N o t e : Divide the dough in half and roll out to 2 smaller rectangles, if desired.

Olive and Pine Nut Bread

MAKES 1 LARGE OR 2 SMALL LOAVES

This loaf has a lovely nutty flavor, and I often serve it with Marinated Goat Cheese (page 12).

Blend the yeast with the water, sugar, and ½ cup all-purpose flour. Leave in a warm place for 10 minutes until frothy.

Mix the remaining flour with the salt and oregano in a large bowl. Make a well in the center and work in the frothed yeast mixture and olive oil to form a soft dough. Knead the dough for 8 minutes, then add the olives and pine nuts. Continue to knead for a further 2 minutes, adding a little extra flour to help incorporate the olives and nuts, if necessary.

Place the dough in a lightly oiled bowl, turning once to coat the surface. Cover and

Ingredients

1¼ teaspoons active dry yeast
1¼ cups tepid water
Pinch of sugar
1½ cups all-purpose flour
1½ cups whole wheat flour
1 teaspoon salt
1 teaspoon dried oregano
¼ cup extra-virgin olive oil
¾ cup pitted black olives
⅓ cup pine nuts

let rise in a warm place for 35 to 40 minutes, or until doubled in size.

Preheat the oven to 425°F. and lightly oil a large baking sheet.

Punch the dough down on a lightly floured surface, being careful not to lose any olives or nuts, and shape into 1 large or 2 small rounds. Place on the prepared baking sheet, brush lightly with oil, cover, and let rise for a further 25 to 30 minutes.

Transfer to the oven and bake for 35 to 40 minutes, or until the crust is golden. Transfer to a wire rack to cool completely.

Sun-Dried Tomato and Parmesan Bread

MAKES 1 LOAF

This is a rich and tasty rolled, stuffed bread in which the flavors of the filling permeate the dough. Roll the dough up tightly, since the filling tends to fall out if rolled too loosely. Sun-dried tomatoes have a highly concentrated tomato flavor, and are available either in oil or dried. If dried, reconstitute by soaking in boiling water for 5 minutes until soft. Drain well and continue as directed.

Ingredients

DOUGH	STUFFING
1¼ teaspoons active dry yeast	1 tablespoon olive oil
1¼ cups tepid water	1 small onion, finely chopped
1 teaspoon sugar	1 teaspoon chopped fresh rosemary
3 cups all-purpose flour	1 teaspoon fennel seeds
1 teaspoon salt	⅓ cup sun-dried tomatoes in oil, drained and finely chopped
2 tablespoons (¼ stick) butter	½ cup freshly grated Parmesan cheese

Blend the yeast with the water, sugar, and ½ cup flour and set aside in a warm place for 10 minutes, until frothy.

Sift the remaining flour and salt into a large bowl and rub in the butter. Make a well in the center and work in the frothed yeast mixture to form a soft dough. Knead for 8 to 10 minutes, or until the dough is smooth and elastic. Place in an oiled bowl, turning once to coat the dough, cover, and let rise in a warm place for 35 to 40 minutes, or until doubled in size.

Make the stuffing. Heat the oil in a small skillet and sauté the onion, rosemary, and fennel seeds for 5 minutes, until the onion is soft. Add the tomatoes and stir for 1 minute. Let cool to room temperature.

Punch the dough down on a lightly floured surface and roll out to a rectangle approximately 10 × 12 inches. Brush the surface with a little oil and sprinkle over the stuffing, leaving a narrow border around the edge. Top with the Parmesan and roll up the dough tightly from one short end, like a jelly roll.

Preheat the oven to 425°F. and lightly oil a large baking sheet.

Transfer the dough to the prepared baking sheet, seam side down, pressing the ends under to enclose the stuffing completely. Brush the dough with a little oil, cover, and set aside in a warm place for 25 to 30 minutes more, until nearly doubled in bulk.

Bake for 35 minutes, or until the crust is golden. Cool on a wire rack.

Note: This bread is my favorite among the recipes included in this book. Although it is best eaten the day it is made, I often toast any leftovers to serve with soups or salads.

For a tasty alternative, spread the rolled-out dough with 2 tablespoons of olive paste before adding the cooled tomato mixture and then continue as directed.

Seeded Cornmeal Soda Rolls

MAKES 6 ROLLS

Baking soda is used as the rising agent in this adaptation of classic Irish soda bread.
I was inspired to make my own version after visiting Ballymaloe House, in Cork, Ireland, which
is famous for its delicious breads. Sesame and sunflower seeds and cornmeal are added to the flour
and the dough is shaped into rolls before baking. The resulting bread is deliciously savory and
makes a good accompaniment to soups. Try it with Red Pepper Soup (page 32).

Ingredients

2½ cups all-purpose flour
⅔ cup finely ground yellow
cornmeal
1 teaspoon baking soda
1 teaspoon salt
4 tablespoons (½ stick) butter
¼ cup sesame seeds
¼ cup sunflower seeds
½ cup milk
½ cup plain yogurt

Preheat the oven to 425°F. and lightly oil 1 large baking sheet.

In a large bowl combine the flour, cornmeal, baking soda, and salt and rub in the butter until the mixture resembles fine bread crumbs. Stir in all but 1 teaspoon of the sesame seeds and all but 1 teaspoon of the sunflower seeds. Work in the milk and yogurt to form a stiff dough.

Shape the dough into 6 equal-size rolls, cut a cross in the top of each with a sharp knife, and brush with a little milk. Sprinkle the reserved seeds on top.

Place the rolls on the prepared baking sheet, approximately 3 to 4 inches apart, and bake for 25 to 30 minutes, until the rolls are risen and golden. Let cool on a wire rack.

Walnut and Poppy Seed Loaf

MAKES 2 LOAVES

This moist, nutty bread is wonderful for sandwiches. It also toasts very well and can be spread with either sweet or savory toppings.

Blend the yeast with the water, sugar, and ½ cup flour. Leave in a warm place for 10 minutes, until frothy.

Place the remaining flour and salt in a large bowl and stir in the walnuts and 2 tablespoons of the poppy seeds. Make a well in the center and work in the frothed yeast mixture, milk, and butter to form a soft dough. Knead for 8 to 10 minutes, or until the dough is smooth and elastic. Place in an oiled bowl, turning once to coat the dough. Cover and let rise in a warm place for 35 to 40 minutes, until doubled in size.

Ingredients

1 package active dry yeast
(1 scant tablespoon)
1¼ cups tepid water
1 teaspoon sugar
4 cups whole wheat flour
1 teaspoon salt
¾ cup shelled walnuts, finely chopped
3 tablespoons poppy seeds
⅔ cup tepid milk
3 tablespoons butter, melted

Preheat the oven to 450°F. and lightly oil two 9×5-inch loaf pans.

Punch the dough down on a lightly floured surface. Divide in half, and shape each half into an oval loaf and place in a prepared pan. Brush the surface with a little oil, cover, and let dough rise for a further 25 to 30 minutes, or until it just reaches the top of each pan.

Brush the surface of each loaf carefully with a little milk and sprinkle over the remaining poppy seeds. Bake for 30 to 35 minutes, until risen and golden.

Turn the bread out of the pans and let cool on a wire rack.

Desserts

Pear and Blackberry Sorbet with Vodka

Having made this sorbet several times, I had been struggling to come up with a sauce to do it justice. Then in a flash of inspiration, I tried it with a dash of vodka. It was the perfect combination, enhancing the flavors of the sorbet while adding an extra dimension to the dish.

Ingredients

PEAR SORBET	BLACKBERRY SORBET
1½ pounds firm ripe pears, such as Bosc or Bartlett, peeled, cored, and quartered	1 pound blackberries, defrosted if frozen
1 cup water	Juice of 1 lemon
¼ cup dessert wine, such as Sauternes	1¼ cups sugar
4 cardamom pods, bruised	1 cup water
Juice of ½ lemon	Chilled vodka to serve
1 cup sugar	Extra blackberries and mint or lemon balm leaves, for garnish

Line a 9 × 5-inch loaf pan with plastic wrap.

Put the pears, water, wine, cardamom, and lemon juice in a 2-quart saucepan and bring to a boil. Cover and simmer over low heat for 10 minutes, or until the pears are tender. Remove the pears with a slotted spoon and puree until smooth. Place in a bowl and let cool.

Strain the cooking liquid into a clean saucepan and carefully add the sugar. Let it dissolve over low heat, without stirring, then bring to a boil and cook over high heat for 3 minutes. Remove from the heat and let cool completely.

Puree the blackberries with the lemon juice and pass through a fine sieve to remove the seeds. Dissolve the sugar in the water as above and set aside until completely cooled.

When both syrups are completely cool, stir in their respective fruit purees. Pour the fruit syrups into separate plastic containers and place in the freezer. Freeze both mixtures until firm around the edges and then beat well to break up any ice crystals. Repeat this twice more and leave until frozen.

Remove the pear sorbet from the freezer, allow to soften slightly, and press into the prepared loaf pan. Smooth the surface and return to the freezer until firm.

Remove the blackberry sorbet from the freezer, allow to soften slightly, and press on top of the pear layer. Smooth the surface and freeze until completely firm, several hours or overnight.

To serve the sorbet, remove from the freezer and allow to soften for 10 to 20 minutes in the refrigerator. Flood each serving plate with a little vodka, remove the sorbet from the refrigerator, turn out onto a cutting board, peel away the plastic wrap, and cut into slices. Place a slice in the center of each plate and garnish with extra blackberries and mint leaves, if desired. Serve immediately.

Golden Fruit Salad

SERVES 6

Good fruit salads are worth their weight in gold, and provide the perfect end to any dinner party. This one is both attractive and delicious, with its combination of golden fruit, spices, and mint.

Ingredients

1½ pounds chopped mixed fruits
(cherries, mangos, nectarines,
papayas, peaches, plums,
red grapes, strawberries)
2 ruby grapefruits
4 teaspoons honey

½ teaspoon ground cinnamon
¼ teaspoon ground cloves
Pinch of freshly grated nutmeg
1 tablespoon shredded fresh mint
Mint leaves, for garnish

Place the prepared fruits in a large bowl.

Over a small bowl, peel and segment the grape-fruits. Add the segments to the other fruit and squeeze out all the juice from the skins and membrane. Stir in the honey and spices and pour over the fruit.

Chill for 15 minutes in the refrigerator, then serve scattered with mint leaves.

SERVES 6–8

I have always been a passionate lover of the traditional tarte Tatin, *the upside-down French apple tart invented by the Tatin sisters. I have adapted the recipe by using bananas instead of apples. They are baked in a skillet in the oven under a rich pastry blanket. When cooked, the tart is turned upside down to reveal a succulent layer of caramelized bananas.*

To make the pastry, sift the flour and salt into a bowl and rub in the butter until the mixture resembles fine bread crumbs. Stir in the almonds and sugar, then work in the egg yolk and 2 tablespoons cold water to form a soft dough. Add the remaining water if the dough is too firm. Cover and refrigerate for 30 minutes.

Preheat the oven to 425°F.

For the topping, heat the butter in an 8-inch skillet or flameproof baking dish. Stir in the brown sugar and cook over medium heat for 5 minutes. Peel the bananas and cut in half lengthwise. Place in the pan cut side up and continue to cook for 3 to 4 minutes, until the bananas begin to brown underneath.

Ingredients

PASTRY
1¼ cups all-purpose flour
½ teaspoon salt
6 tablespoons (¾ stick) unsalted butter, diced
¼ cup ground almonds
2 teaspoons granulated sugar
1 egg yolk
2 to 3 tablespoons cold water

TOPPING
8 tablespoons (1 stick) unsalted butter
½ cup soft light brown sugar
6 medium ripe but firm bananas

Crème fraîche or plain yogurt

Remove the dough from the refrigerator and roll out to a circle a little larger than the skillet, about ¼ inch thick. Lay the dough over the bananas to cover them completely, pressing the edges up the sides of the pan. Work fast to avoid softening the dough with the heat.

Transfer the pan to the oven and bake for 20 minutes, until the pastry is golden. Remove from the oven and let rest in the pan for 5 minutes, before turning out onto a serving dish large enough to contain the cooking juices.

Serve the tart warm or cold, garnished with crème fraîche or plain yogurt, as preferred.

Spiced Stuffed Pears with Buttery Apple Sauce

SERVES 4

A delicious combination of flavors in the filling for these pears makes this an unusual and exquisite dessert. It is served with a caramelized apple sauce, which complements the spiced pears very well.

Ingredients

FILLING
½ cup (4 ounces) ricotta
⅓ cup dried apricots, finely chopped
¼ cup preserved ginger in syrup, finely chopped
1 tablespoon pine nuts, toasted
1 tablespoon lemon juice
¼ teaspoon ground cinnamon

4 large pears
Extra lemon juice

APPLE SAUCE
¼ cup sugar
2 tablespoons water
Juice of ½ lemon
1 tablespoon Calvados or brandy
⅓ cup apple juice
4 tablespoons (½ stick) unsalted butter, diced

Preheat the oven to 375°F.

Place the ricotta in a bowl and beat in the apricots, ginger, syrup, pine nuts, lemon juice, and cinnamon until combined. Set aside.

Peel the pears and scoop out the cores from the base ends, being careful not to cut right through the fruit. Slice a thin piece from the base of each pear so it will sit flat and brush liberally, inside and out, with lemon juice.

Divide the filling among the pears and stuff into the hollow centers, pressing firmly. Set the pears in an ovenproof dish and cover with aluminum foil. Transfer to the oven and bake for 20 to 25 minutes, until the pears are tender. Remove from the oven.

While the pears are cooking, prepare the sauce. Place the sugar and water in a small, heavy-bottomed saucepan and heat gently until the sugar is dissolved. Bring to a boil and let bubble until the syrup begins to caramelize and turn golden, about 5 minutes. Be careful not to let the syrup become too brown or it will taste bitter. Remove from the heat and whisk in the lemon juice, Calvados, and apple juice. Return to the heat. Bring back to a boil and cook over high heat for 2 to 3 minutes to reduce slightly.

Whisk in the butter, a little at a time, to make a smooth and glossy sauce. Cool slightly.

Cut the pears into slices and drizzle a little sauce over them before serving.

Chocolate Mousse Terrine with Pistachio Sauce

SERVES 10–12

This dessert is a chocolate-lover's dream come true. Three sumptuous layers of chocolate mousse, all with slightly different textures, are set in a terrine and served with a creamy pistachio sauce. It's wickedly indulgent! You may need to use a warmed knife to slice through the delicate layers. If you like, make the chocolate leaves in advance and store them in an airtight container. Start this dish the day before you plan to serve it.

Ingredients

SEMISWEET CHOCOLATE MOUSSE
6 ounces semisweet chocolate
2 tablespoons (¼ stick) unsalted butter
4 tablespoons heavy cream
1 tablespoon brandy
1 egg, separated

MILK CHOCOLATE MOUSSE
6 ounces milk chocolate
4 tablespoons (½ stick) unsalted butter

2 tablespoons heavy cream
1 tablespoon brandy
1 egg, separated

WHITE CHOCOLATE MOUSSE
8 ounces white chocolate
6 tablespoons (¾ stick) unsalted butter
2 tablespoons heavy cream
1 tablespoon brandy
1 egg, separated

Line a 9 × 5-inch loaf pan with plastic wrap.

Put the semisweet chocolate, butter, cream, and brandy in a small bowl and place over a pan of gently simmering water. Heat until the chocolate and butter are melted, then stir well. Let cool slightly, then beat in the egg yolk. In a separate bowl, whisk the egg white until stiff and carefully fold into the chocolate mixture. Pour into the prepared loaf pan and refrigerate for several hours, until set.

Repeat the above method, first with the milk chocolate and then with the white chocolate, ensuring that each layer is firmly set before adding the next. Let the terrine set completely in the refrigerator overnight.

Meanwhile, make the pistachio sauce. Heat the milk and vanilla bean in a 1-quart saucepan until just boiling. Remove from the heat and infuse for 10 minutes. Remove the vanilla bean and reserve for another use.

continued

Pistachio Sauce

Ingredients

2½ cups milk
1 vanilla bean
6 egg yolks
½ cup sugar
1 cup shelled pistachio nuts,
peeled and ground
4 tablespoons heavy cream

CHOCOLATE LEAVES
(Optional)
1 ounce semisweet or milk chocolate
10 to 12 rose leaves

Extra cream and semisweet chocolate

Beat the egg yolks and sugar in a large bowl until pale and creamy. Beat in the vanilla-flavored milk and pass through a fine sieve into a clean saucepan. Place over low heat and stir the mixture with a wooden spoon until it thickens slightly and coats the back of the spoon. Do not allow the sauce to boil or it will curdle. Stir in the pistachio nuts and let infuse overnight. Pass through a sieve and stir in the cream. Set aside.

At this point you can make the chocolate leaves, if you like. Melt chocolate of your choice. Wash and dry the rose leaves. Using a small paint brush, coat the underside of the leaves with a thick layer of chocolate, being careful not to get any on the other side. Let dry and solidify on wax paper for several hours. Carefully peel the leaves away from the chocolate. Store chocolate leaves in a cool place until required.

Tint a spoonful of cream to a light shade of brown with a little melted semisweet chocolate and set aside.

To serve the terrine, remove from the refrigerator and turn out onto a cutting board. Peel away the plastic wrap and cut into slices with a slightly warmed knife. Flood each plate with a little sauce, place a slice of terrine in the center, and garnish with a chocolate leaf. Place a few drops of plain and chocolate-colored cream around the sauce and, with a toothpick, draw a line through each one to form a heart-shaped pattern.

Serve at once.

Elderflower and Strawberry Syllabub

SERVES 4

Elderflower syrup is sometimes available at good health food stores. However, if you are unable to find any, substitute a fruit liqueur such as crème de pêche or crème de cassis. Both are equally delicious. I have used yogurt instead of cream for a lighter and more refreshing syllabub.

Ingredients

2 cups yogurt cheese *(page 8)*
8 tablespoons elderflower syrup or fruit liqueur
2 egg whites

12 strawberries, hulled and halved

4 small strawberries and 4 sprigs of lemon balm, for garnish

Place the yogurt cheese in a bowl and stir in 4 tablespoons of syrup or liqueur. Beat the egg whites until stiff and carefully fold into the mixture until just combined.

Place the strawberries in 4 tall glasses and divide the remaining syrup or liqueur among them. Carefully spoon in the syllabub mixture and place the glasses in the refrigerator to chill for 1 hour.

Decorate each syllabub with a strawberry and a sprig of lemon balm.

Individual Hazelnut Meringue Gateaux

SERVES 4

A great friend and mentor of mine first served me a delicious nut meringue gateau with raspberries, and I was totally hooked. Here the meringue is piped to make small circles and layered with cream and raspberries to be served as individual gateaux. Assemble the layers about thirty minutes before serving—this allows the bottom two layers to become gooey while the top layer remains crisp.

N o t e : You will need a piping bag fitted with a ¼-inch plain nozzle.

Ingredients

MERINGUE
3 egg whites
¾ cup granulated sugar
1 teaspoon cornstarch
⅔ cup shelled hazelnuts, toasted and finely ground

FILLING
¾ cup heavy cream
2 tablespoons Grand Marnier
1 tablespoon superfine sugar
4 cups fresh raspberries

TOPPING
⅓ cup sliced almonds, toasted
Confectioners' sugar, for dusting

Draw twelve 4-inch circles on a sheet of wax paper to act as templates, and brush well with oil. Place on a large baking sheet.

Preheat the oven to 300°F.

Whisk the egg whites in a large bowl until stiff, then gradually beat in the sugar, a tablespoon at a time. The mixture will be thick and glossy. Fold in the cornstarch and ground hazelnuts. Spoon the mixture into the piping bag and pipe over the templates, starting in the center and working outwards, to make 12 meringue circles.

Transfer to the oven and bake for 1¾ to 2 hours, or until the meringues have dried out thoroughly. Remove from the oven and cool completely on the paper. When completely cool, carefully peel off the paper.

About 30 minutes before serving, whip the cream, Grand Marnier, and sugar together until stiff and spread over 8 of the meringue circles. Top all 8 with raspberries. Assemble the 4 gateaux with 2 layers each of meringue, raspberries, and cream, topped with a final layer of meringue. Refrigerate for 30 minutes. Sprinkle the almonds over the top, dust lightly with the confectioners' sugar, and serve.

Caribbean Cooler

My husband spent some time working in the Caribbean and on his return asked me to make him ice cream with mangos, a dish that he'd tasted and loved. This recipe gained his approval.

Heat the coconut milk in a 1-quart saucepan until it just reaches the boiling point. In a large bowl, beat the egg yolks with the sugar until pale. Whisk in the hot milk and strain into a clean saucepan. Stir over low heat until the mixture thickens and coats the back of the spoon. Do not allow the mixture to boil or it will curdle. Remove from the heat and pour into a large bowl. Let cool completely.

Puree the mango with the lemon juice until smooth and stir into the cooled coconut custard until combined. Freeze until firm.

Ingredients

ICE CREAM
1½ cups unsweetened coconut milk
6 egg yolks
¾ cup sugar
2 mangos,
peeled and pits removed
Juice of 1 lemon

BASKETS
4 tablespoons (½ stick) butter
4 tablespoons sugar
2 tablespoons honey
4 tablespoons all-purpose flour
1 teaspoon ground cinnamon

Preheat the oven to 375°F. and lightly oil a large baking sheet.

Prepare the baskets. Place the butter, sugar, and honey in a small saucepan and heat gently until the butter melts. Remove from the heat and stir in the flour and cinnamon.

Place 2 tablespoons of the mixture, well apart, on the prepared baking sheet. With the back of a wetted spoon, spread the mixture out to form an oval, approximately 3 × 2 inches. Bake for 5 to 6 minutes, or until golden and well spread.

Remove from the oven, cool slightly, and carefully peel from the baking sheet. Let cool over the handle of a rolling pin in the shape of a canoe. Repeat twice to make 6 canoe baskets.

When the ice cream is frozen and you are ready to serve it, allow to soften for 10 minutes or so. Place 2 to 3 scoops in each basket and serve immediately.

Fresh Berry Mousse

SERVES 6

There are so many wonderful fresh berries available at the markets these days that this mousse can be made almost all year round. However, it will be at its best during the summer months. If you get the chance, there is nothing more enjoyable than picking your own berries, fresh from the hedgerows and woods.

Reserve a few of each kind of berry for decoration. Place the rest in a blender or food processor and puree until smooth. Press through a fine sieve to remove all the seeds. You should have 1–1¼ cups of puree. Stir in the honey and port.

Whip the cream until it holds its shape and gradually beat it into the puree.

Ingredients

1 pound mixed hulled summer berries, including strawberries, raspberries, boysenberries, loganberries, and blackberries
⅓ cup honey
¼ cup ruby port
1 cup heavy cream
3 egg whites

Beat the egg whites until stiff and carefully fold into the mixture. Divide the mousse among 6 serving dishes or wine glasses and chill for at least 2 hours.

Decorate each portion with a few of the reserved berries and serve while still chilled with a selection of sweet biscuits or cookies.

Appendix

Conversions

Ingredients and Equipment Glossary

British English and American English are not always the same, particularly in the kitchen. The following ingredients and equipment used in this book are pretty much the same on both sides of the Atlantic, but just have different names.

AMERICAN	BRITISH
apple cider	non-alcoholic sweet-tart apple juice
arugula	rocket
baking soda	bicarbonate of soda
beans (dried)— lima, navy, Great Northern	dried white (haricot) beans
Belgian endive	chicory
bell pepper	sweet pepper (capsicum)
Bibb and Boston lettuce	soft-leaved, round lettuce
broiler/to broil	grill/to grill
celery stalk	celery stick
celery root	celeriac
cheesecloth	muslin
chile	chili
confectioners' sugar	icing sugar
cookie cutter	biscuit or pastry cutter
cornstarch	cornflour
crushed hot red pepper	dried crushed red chili
eggplant	aubergine
escarole	batavia
fava bean	broad bean
fresh ginger	fresh root ginger
golden raisins	sultanas
half-and-half	single cream
hard cider	cider (alcoholic)
heavy cream (37.6% fat)	double cream (35–40% fat)
kitchen towel	tea towel
pancake	griddle cake
snow pea	mange-tout
parchment paper	non-stick baking paper
peanut oil	groundnut oil
pearl onion	button or baby onion
romaine lettuce	cos lettuce
scallion	spring onion
semisweet chocolate	plain chocolate
skillet	frying pan
superfine sugar	use caster sugar
tomato puree	sieved tomatoes or pasatta
vanilla bean	vanilla pod
whole milk	homogenized milk
zucchini	courgette

Volume Equivalents

These are not exact equivalents for the American cups and spoons, but have been rounded up or down slightly to make measuring easier.

AMERICAN MEASURES	METRIC	IMPERIAL
¼ t	1.25 ml	
½ t	2.5 ml	
1 t	5 ml	
½ T (1½ t)	7.5 ml	
1 T (3 t)	15 ml	
¼ cup (4 T)	60 ml	2 fl oz
⅓ cup (5 T)	75 ml	2½ fl oz
½ cup (8 T)	125 ml	4 fl oz
⅔ cup (10 T)	150 ml	5 fl oz (¼ pint)
¾ cup (12 T)	175 ml	6 fl oz
1 cup (16 T)	250 ml	8 fl oz
1¼ cups	300 ml	10 fl oz (½ pint)
1½ cups	350 ml	12 fl oz
1 pint (2 cups)	500 ml	16 fl oz
1 quart (4 cups)	1 litre	1¾ pints

Weight Equivalents

The metric weights given in this chart are not exact equivalents, but have been rounded up or down slightly to make measuring easier.

AVOIRDUPOIS		METRIC	
¼	oz	7	g
½	oz	15	g
1	oz	30	g
2	oz	60	g
3	oz	90	g
4	oz	115	g
5	oz	150	g
6	oz	175	g
7	oz	200	g
8	oz (½ lb)	225	g
9	oz	250	g
10	oz	300	g
11	oz	325	g
12	oz	350	g
13	oz	375	g
14	oz	400	g
15	oz	425	g
1	lb	450	g
1	lb 2 oz	500	g
1½	lb	750	g
2	lb	900	g
2¼	lb	1	kg
3	lb	1.4	kg
4	lb	1.8	kg
4½	lb	2	kg

Oven Temperature Equivalents

OVEN	°F.	°C.	GAS MARK
very cool	250–275	130–140	½–1
cool	300	150	2
warm	325	170	3
moderate	350	180	4
moderately hot	375	190	5
	400	200	6
hot	425	220	7
very hot	450	230	8
	475	250	9

Butter

Some confusion may arise over the measuring of butter and other hard fats. In the United States, butter is generally sold in a one-pound package, which contains four equal "sticks." The wrapper on each stick is marked to show tablespoons, so the cook can cut the stick according to the quantity required. The equivalent weights are:

1 stick = 115 g/4 oz
1 tablespoon = 15 g/½ oz

Eggs

American eggs are graded slightly differently than British eggs. Here are the equivalent sizes:

extra large egg (64 g) =
  size 2 (65 g)
large egg (57 g) =
  size 3 (60 g) or 4 (55 g)
medium egg (50 g) =
  size 5 (50 g)

Flour

American all-purpose flour is milled from a mixture of hard and soft wheats, whereas British plain flour is made mainly from soft wheat. To achieve a near equivalent to American all-purpose flour, use half British plain flour and half strong bread flour.

Sugar

In the recipes in this book, if sugar is called for it is assumed to be granulated, unless otherwise specified. American granulated sugar is finer than British granulated, closer to caster sugar. Other than in preserves recipes, where British granulated or preserving sugar can be used if preferred, caster sugar should be substituted throughout.

Yeast

Quantities of dried yeast (called active dry yeast in the United States) are usually given in number of packages. Each of these packages contains 7 g/¼ oz of yeast, which is equivalent to a scant tablespoon.

Index

Design by Lynn Pieroni

Composed in Centaur with QuarkXpress 3.0 on a Macintosh IIsi
by Barbara Sturman at Stewart, Tabori & Chang, New York, New York.
Output on a Linotronic L300 at The Sarabande Press, New York, New York.

Printed and bound by Toppan Printing Company, Ltd.,
Tokyo, Japan.